CARL JUNG

CARL JUNG

THE PSYCHOANALYST WHO UNCOVERED THE SECRETS OF THE MIND

LILY YUAN

Picture Credits:
Alamy: 36, 40, 55, 112
Bridgeman Images: 61, 149
Diomedia: 79, 96
Getty Images: 85
Library of Congress: 101, 103, 145
Patricia Kucmanova: 90, 92
Shutterstock: 16, 25, 99, 107, 124, 127
Wellcome Collection: 48, 65, 74
Wikimedia Commons: 9, 29, 33, 43, 46, 51, 57, 69, 97, 110, 116, 122, 142, 156

This edition published in 2024 by Arcturus Publishing Limited
26/27 Bickels Yard, 151–153 Bermondsey Street,
London SE1 3HA

AD011366UK

Printed in the UK

CONTENTS

CHAPTER 1

INTRODUCTION TO CARL JUNG AND HIS FOUR STAGES OF LIFE

Carl Gustav Jung. The psychiatric mastermind and worldwide phenomenon behind archetypes, personality types and dream analysis. The man who boldly brought analytic psychology into light. He's often depicted as a calm, quiet thinker with iconic circle lenses in a pensive stance. Paired with a cheeky grin.

Many know his quotes, but few understand his story. What happened during his lifetime? Who did he encounter? Where did he travel to? What was the motivation behind his actions? When exactly were the pivotal (and lesser told) points in his life? And of course, why did he turn out the way he did?

Jung's life journey was anything but straightforward. From having a curiosity for a wide range of subjects to his wild encounters with his psychiatric patients, he trekked a path no man during his time had dared to venture before. Through the murky waters of the subconscious to the peaks and valleys of his emotions, Jung was an iconoclast in the finest sense of the word.

With his off-beaten path came excruciating lengths of suffering, guilt and shame – and an everlasting legacy. To this day, Jung is quoted in textbooks, lectures and every psychology course to exist in the 21st century. Without Jung, psychology would be a completely different discipline.

Jung identified four stages of life: Childhood, Youth, Middle Life, and Old Age in his essay 'The Stages of Life' from *The Structure and Dynamics of the Psyche* (1931). He compared these stages to the position of the sun in the sky – from dusk until dawn – with the brightest time being the middle of one's life.

More specifically, the brightness of the sun represented consciousness. This book will take a detailed and eye-opening journey through Jung's life via his own lens, with important people and events that shaped his worldview. All of Jung's personal quotes are *italicized* and included in boxes for easy reference.

In addition, Jung posited the eight distinct psychological types in 1921. At the core of Jung's personality theory is the fundamental dichotomy of introversion and extraversion. He proposed that individuals prefer an energy orientation – either inward (introversion) or outward (extraversion). Introverts tend to focus on their inner thoughts and experiences, while extraverts are more oriented towards the external world and social interactions.

Building on this foundation, Jung identified four psychological functions that describe how individuals process information: Thinking, Feeling, Sensation and Intuition.

Thinking involves intellectual processing and decision-making based on logic, while Feeling involves decisions based on values and emotions. Sensation pertains to the reception of information through the senses and awareness of concrete details, and Intuition involves perceiving information in an abstract, intuitive manner, often focusing on possibilities and potential future scenarios.

A portrait of Carl Jung, c.1916.

Often the hands know how to solve a riddle with which the intellect has wrestled in vain.

Culture lies outside the purpose of nature. Could by any chance culture be the meaning and purpose of the second half of life?

CHILDHOOD

To begin with, let's introduce the first of the four stages of life, according to Jung – Childhood:

Jung proposed three substages in Childhood: anarchic (archetypal), monarchic (ego) and dualistic (socialization). A child gains consciousness when he or she *knows* that an object or person exists. During the entire developmental period before puberty, children are governed by instinct (*I want*) as opposed to a superego (*we should*). When a child learns to share, they move away from only having an id.

The id is the primitive, instinctual part of the psyche. It operates on the pleasure principle, seeking immediate gratification of basic needs and desires, without concern for consequences or social norms. The id is considered unconscious and present from birth, and represents innate biological drives and impulses.

In contrast, the superego represents the moral compass of the psyche. It acts as a conscience, and strives for moral consistency, and works hard subconsciously to restrain the impulses of the id, which may land someone in hot water. The superego develops as a person grows and is heavily influenced and shaped by cultural and societal norms.

The anarchic state consists of chaotic 'islands' of consciousness prone to entropy, and primitive images. Infants at this point are in a state of 'participation mystique', in which they are closely connected to the collective unconscious and have a limited sense of differentiation between themselves and the world around them. Life is simply a collection of experiences and sensations without memories.

Children who are still in their unconscious state exist in a vacuum known (the participation mystique mentioned above), where they live in a psychological unity with their parents' unconscious. During Jung's sessions with young patients, he would frequently analyse the dreams of the child's parents. Through this, he suggested the child's early struggles may be caused by the unlived lives of their parents.

When the ego and self-awareness begins to form, that's when children enter the monarchic stage, around age four. They recognize at this stage that they have an identity, and are able to form their first memories.

Their development of spoken language comprehension (e.g. full sentences) happens around this time as well. This is when they gain 'consciousness' and are aware of their existence. The 'islands' of consciousness expand, and children begin to understand logical thinking.

Finally, as children begin to understand and separate themselves as individuals, around the age of six, they enter the dualistic stage. At this point, they form relationships outside of their immediate family and effectively learn how to adapt to the demands of their social environment. Such is the survival instinct; no man (or child) is an island.

Concurrently, their cognitive abilities progress, enabling a more nuanced understanding of social dynamics. As they navigate this dualistic stage, children cultivate the capacity to empathize with their peers and comprehend the diverse viewpoints that exist within their expanding social sphere.

In this context, the school environment becomes a significant arena for social learning, providing a structured setting for children to engage with peers, negotiate social hierarchies, and refine their interpersonal skills. Children who have been home-schooled may miss out on certain critical aspects of social development – which may result in awkwardness in Youth.

Some children, Jung suggests, have a 'congenital sensitiveness' that increases the likelihood of them adopting a neurotic attitude later on. The islands have now become one continuous landmass. Their thoughts in their little brains begin to take form and properly congregate to make sense.

Jung has spoken on the many challenges and pivotal points of Childhood, and placed a strong emphasis on parental upbringing:

> *The greatest burden a child must bear is the unlived life of its parents.*

> *The creation of something new is not accomplished by the intellect but by the play instinct.*

Jung posited that when a child enters this world, they arrive as a highly intricate being with inherent traits that persist throughout their lifetime. These inborn characteristics often catch parents by surprise, leading to astonishment within the family when their child's personality proves to be drastically different from their own and, at times, appears strikingly unfamiliar.

These distinctions, alien to both parents and even siblings, often serve as the origins of family misunderstandings and conflicts. The child (largely unconsciously) learns strategies to obtain what they desire, whether that would be their favourite sweet, a trip to the zoo, or even the praise of a certain caregiver.

Jung believed that every child should be regarded as a fresh experiment in the continuous flux of life, an endeavour to find a novel solution or adaptation. As a distinct and original individual, the child must remain true to their inherent nature, compelling parents to acknowledge their child's unique essence to guide them towards an existence that is genuine and authentic.

YOUTH

The end of puberty marks the beginning of Youth, which is defined by the inevitable end of Childhood, and 'psychic birth' of personality. Youth requires many more responsibilities to become a fully fledged, functional citizen of society. They must learn what strengths and skills they can offer.

Youth adapts to the world as the child develops an ego. It marks the beginning of a journey to independence and self-understanding, especially with regards to the shadow (the hidden, guilt-ridden side to an individual's personality). They begin the grand process of individuation – the starting point of developing a personality unique to the individual. Individuation is a process of psychological growth and self-discovery that involves integrating the conscious and unconscious aspects of the self.

Individuals in the Youth stage often engage in a process of self-discovery and identity formation. They may experiment with different roles, values and belief systems to understand who they are and what they stand for. They mingle with different social groups, adopt a new fashion style every week, and cycle through various music playlists.

Puberty is the juncture at which the psyche solidifies into a tangible entity, a phenomenon designated by Jung as psychic birth. This period is characterized by challenges that necessitate adaptation, requiring the cessation of childhood fantasies and the confrontation of the pragmatic demands of adulthood. During this phase, attention is primarily directed outwards, with a prevailing consciousness as people strive to attain their objectives and carve out a stable and prosperous niche for themselves in the world.

Young adults strive for greater independence from their parents and other authority figures. They may move away from home, pursue higher education or start their careers, and make decisions that shape their own lives. They learn how to manage their finances, harness their autonomy, and adjust the sails to their own boats on their journey as they move through the unconscious seas of thought.

As they form their own identities, individuals in the Youth stage may question and re-evaluate the values and beliefs they were raised with. They may adopt new values or modify existing ones to align with their emerging sense of self. An individual in the Youth growth stage may reject previously learned religious values, for example, and replace them with a newfound sense of agnosticism.

The young person, whether man or woman, is still the developing creature who, in the sense of the archetype of the hero, is preparing to become the warrior and accomplish the deed that will prove their worth.

Some common collective goals are to find a partner with whom to have a family and to make a mark on the world. When people enter Youth, they sow seeds for the future. They still enjoy the moment and relish spontaneity but recognize the importance of planning for the future.

Becoming financially self-sufficient and responsible is an important aspect of the Youth stage. Individuals may secure employment, manage finances and make financial decisions for themselves. Gone are the days when their parents (or primary caregivers) would tell them what activities to engage in or what to wear.

People who have integrated successfully into the season of Youth often have multiple roles they honour, within the spheres of their professional affiliations and personal partnerships. They understand their unique strengths and areas for improvement, in order to become their highest, most fulfilled self.

The Eternal Child Archetype

Many problems occur when someone wishes to remain a child forever, which pop psychology has coined the 'Peter Pan' syndrome. Inner conflicts can happen when someone wants to cling on to their childhood and hence never fully integrate into the stage of Youth. Jung warned the process of integrating into Youth can be hindered through 'exaggerated expectations, underestimation of difficulties, unjustified optimism, or a negative attitude'.

The myth of the *puer* or *puella aeternus* (Latin for eternal child) depicts a child-god who avoids individuation and struggles to move on to the next stage. Jung warns about significant dream symbols which haunt eternal children - any objects that relate to imprisonment. They are essentially 'jailed' within the constraints of their naivety and wonder.

Jung equates the 'eternal child' in a man as 'an indescribable experience, incongruity, handicap and divine prerogative' which ultimately determines the worthiness of a personality. Although not explicitly stated in psychiatric guidelines or manuals, the immaturity and unwillingness of a person to grow up may be indicative of a larger psychological issue.

Picture cages, chains and bars, to name a few. He compares life itself to a prison for the person who refuses to mature and progress to the next season in their life. The eternal child relishes in the comfort of the present instead of facing the challenges that would allow them to undergo a metamorphosis to the next chapter of their life.

Jung's concept of the eternal child has gained recognition as 'Peter Pan' syndrome in popular psychology.

The puer's shadow is the senex (Old Man), associated with the god Apollo – disciplined, controlled, responsible, rational, ordered. Conversely, the shadow of the senex is the puer, related to Dionysus – unbounded instinct, disorder, intoxication, whimsy.

What did Jung have to say about fatherhood and the tremendous amount of responsibility it entails? When he first became a father, he was shocked at how different life became. Although he still held on dearly to his researcher role, he knew his children would require most of his physical and mental energy during their formative years.

Jung suggested that the less one comprehends the goals pursued by their fathers and forefathers, the more they undermine their understanding of themselves. Consequently, they actively contribute to depriving individuals of their roots and guiding instincts, reducing them to mere particles in the mass, governed solely by what Nietzsche termed the spirit of gravity.

He also blatantly stated that in the journey of parenting, each father encounters the potential to influence his daughter's character, leaving the educator, husband or psychiatrist to confront the consequences. The damage caused by the father demands correction from another father, just as the impact of a mother's actions can only be remedied by another mother.

With respect to a father and his son, the father is associated with the 'wise old man' archetype, which emphasizes wisdom, experience and guidance. The father–son relationship is significant in the individuation process because the son must learn how to see himself as an individual entity apart from his father, who'd usually be one of his first (and primary) role models. This character development helps the son find his place in the world.

Of course, the continual individuation process of the father himself must also be taken into consideration as he departs from being the primary 'mentor' figure for his son after he leaves the nest and takes on the responsibility to build a family life of his own. This usually happens around the mid to late twenties of a man's life.

This cyclic recurrence of familial dynamics might be likened to a psychological primordial fault, akin to the enduring curse of the Atrides passed down through successive generations.

> *To be a father is a very difficult task. If only it were limited to providing food, clothing and shelter! That is far from being everything. One must first and foremost know how to grow into a child's soul.*

Energy peaks at this stage, as most people climb the career ladder and acquire professional skills. Jung dubbed late Youth to 'harshly put an end to the dream of childhood', as one's developed ego must face the (often demanding and monotonously predictable) reality. There are bills to be paid, laundry to be done, and a seemingly endless list of errands to run. Welcome to adulthood.

There is no eternal Youth, which ends around 35–40 years of age. At that point, people typically have their career mapped out, and are settled down in terms of their partnership or singledom. They know what steps to take to make progression in their personal, professional and social spheres. On to the next stage...

Thoroughly unprepared, we take the step into the afternoon of life. Worse still, we take this step with the false presupposition that our truths and our ideals will serve us as hitherto.

MIDDLE LIFE

Individuals are most susceptible to drastic personality changes and transformations during Middle Life. It entails great anxiety and depression about the future, as it's when people ask with dejection, 'Is that all there is to life?' They may have spent the first half of their lives saving and working, without questioning the meaning behind their actions. Such are the ruminations that stem from the classic midlife crisis. Separation from a person or career are likely at this stage.

During the midlife crisis, individuals are likely to spontaneously adopt a different style, change their hair drastically, or even move to a new country altogether and chase their unanswered dreams. People at this period in life realize that their time is limited, and they've already spent approximately half of it. What should they do next? What's the ultimate purpose of the seemingly endless circle of working and living?

As individuals move into Middle Life, they begin to confront the fact that they are not invincible and that their time on Earth is limited. They essentially begin to shift their focus from their own personal goals to the larger community and on to the next generation. This can lead to a greater appreciation for life and a sense of urgency to make the most of the time they have left. This can lead to a desire to make a positive impact on the world and leave a lasting legacy.

The decisive question for man is: Is he related to something infinite or not? That is the telling question of his life.

At midlife, the soul asks: 'What have you been doing up until now? What will you do henceforth?'

From around ages 35–40, depression and neuroticism grow, which indicates psychic rigidity. We tend to resist change at this stage, because of the fear of the unknown (not actually death itself). Jung claims that when we fail to innovate, we end up becoming a parody of ourselves. Religion, he suggests, is the school for transitioning into Middle Life – an external code of conduct to understand the sense of meaninglessness life can bring upon us during this stage.

Luckily, there's so much more than doom and gloom during Middle Life. Jung suggested five distinct stages of the midlife transition: accommodation, separation, liminality, reintegration and finally – individuation.

During accommodation, people attempt to balance their persona with external expectations. Then, when they reach separation, they begin to question the degree to which their own values line up with what the world wants from them. After that, people must trek through liminality, the stage where their old persona is rejected and they fight tooth and nail within themselves to create a new one. They can feel restless, bored and are compelled to make impulsive decisions; shooting in the dark and flying wherever the wind blows. When they finally reach reintegration, the tides begin to calm down. And only then can integration begin.

During integration, people adopt a brand new persona and lift a large weight of uncertainty off their backs. They realize which direction their life is headed and start working to achieve their new goals. Finally, the stage of individuation ends the midlife crisis. People understand why the space between their personal values and persona exist and make amends within themselves to carry on their journey with courage.

The sun of consciousness now begins to set...

OLD AGE

Old Age, which begins around the mid-sixties, focuses on a period of reflection largely rooted in the spiritual and philosophical. Jung compares it to the metaphorical sun setting and its rays gradually dimming during dusk. This process represents consciousness dwindling away. An eternal night is just around the corner of a mystical, ephemeral life. Where there is death ... there will be birth, as the cycle of life goes on for generations to come.

Men become women, and women become men. In other words, men become more in touch with feminine values, while women see the benefit in masculine energy. In order to achieve psychological wholeness and fulfilment, individuals need to integrate these aspects of themselves into their conscious awareness. A healthy individual is in touch with both their masculine and feminine sides.

One cannot live the afternoon of life according to the programme of life's morning; for what was great in the morning will be of little importance in the evening, and what in the morning was true will at evening have become a lie.

This process of integration involves recognizing and accepting parts of oneself that may be considered traditionally feminine or masculine. The most significant regrets elders have are rooted in the failure to take advantage of opportunities and simply *act*. Passivity may have felt comfortable in the short term, but the sting is felt later, once the individual is aware of how fast time flies. The sun of consciousness will set soon, as more than half of life has passed by at this point.

Elders may withdraw from the world and focus on their inner lives. This can involve letting go of worldly concerns and focusing on personal growth and reflection. Although pop culture deems this period to be 'the golden years', individuals who are confronted with their aging bodies and minds may go through yet another crisis and sink into despair.

Internal monologues of 'If I had done ... back then ... then I could've been...' replay through their minds. Their health and vitality is now incomparable to what it had been 30 years earlier. Although it is still possible to go back to school and acquire new skills, it now takes significantly more energy and focus to achieve the same results. The clock keeps ticking, and time may feel like it's passing quicker for those in Old Age.

Each person walks through the stages of life to an inevitable death, which Jung suggested they *strive towards* as opposed to shirking away from. To embrace death, by cherishing what has already happened and making the most of what's left. At this stage, it is equally important to have a purpose in life as it is to have one in death. People may have different experiences throughout their lives, but birth and death are universal.

The concept of an afterlife or God ingrains a sense of meaning and hope during one's final years. It serves as the marker for peace and acceptance. Jung claims it is counterproductive to take an empirical approach to death, because the answers will always be blurry – a form of absurdism. The only certain fact is that every person will eventually undergo a physical death, which Jung saw as a comforting fact.

ABOUT JUNG

Jung believed that our consciousness survives physical death and that the psyche continues to exist beyond the body. However, he did not believe in a concrete or specific concept of an afterlife, but rather saw it as a mystery that could not and will not be fully understood or explained by the human mind. Here are some of Jung's recorded thoughts on God throughout his lifetime:

I find it very difficult to say with certainty what I believe. There is so much that one does not know, cannot prove, and that seems to contradict other things. But I feel that behind everything there is a kind of order, a mysterious unity, which gives meaning and purpose to everything.

He believed that the psyche (or soul) is a real and distinct entity that continues to exist after death. He saw the psyche as a fundamental aspect of human existence that is not bound by the physical body, so it can develop and evolve beyond the limits of the physical world. In some ways, it may carry on forever in dimensions beyond our imagination. Transcending reality, so to speak.

Jung cautiously veered away from the view of a traditional, anthropomorphic God and instead saw God as a symbol of the transcendent and numinous aspects of the psyche. Jung believed that the human psyche has a religious or spiritual dimension, and that this dimension is expressed through images and symbols that have deep meaning and significance for individuals and cultures.

As for personality, Jung himself conceptualized the introversion-extraversion, intuition-sensing, and thinking-feeling dimensions – which he elaborated upon in *Psychological Types* (1921). He saw eight distinct personality types, namely: introverted thinkers (INTP/ISTP), introverted feelers (INFP/ISFP), introverted sensors (ISTJ/ISFJ), introverted intuitives (INTJ/INFJ), extraverted thinkers (ESTJ/ENTP), extraverted feelers (ESFJ/ENFJ), extraverted sensors (ESTP/ESFP), and extraverted intuitives (ENTP/ENFP).

His personality theories have lived on and since been developed into various new-age assessments such as the infamous MBTI®, the Keirsey temperaments, as well as the Colour Code. These concepts can be loosely traced back to the four medieval humours, which are Melancholic (Black Bile), Phlegmatic (Phlegm), Sanguine (Blood) and Choleric (Yellow Bile). Jung's catalogue of human behaviour lives on!

Jung also dabbled with various forms of art, such as sculpting, gouache paintings, mandalas, calligraphy and more. Most of his artistic work remained anonymous until his passing, when his creative talents were preserved and recognized. One lesser-known piece is a statue of a bearded man who possessed many arms, which could be symbolic for his multipotentiality. Onlookers may have different interpretations of his work, which is the whole point of art.

Jung's artistic expressions were deeply intertwined with his explorations of the unconscious mind and archetypal symbols. The artwork found in *The Red Book* includes detailed and symbolic illustrations that showcase his journey plunging into the depths of his psyche. This book spanned 16 full years of Jung's life, from 1914 to 1930.

Art, to Jung, was an outlet for emotional expression. He struggled with a myriad of mental health issues and needed a healthy method to vent. The pencils, pens and paint helped him lift the dark clouds from his head and move into sunnier pastures. Where there were feelings, there could be art. And Jung was more than willing to break through any dead-set 'rules' to push through conventional forms of art.

Let's walk through Jung's (own proposed) four stages of life starting from his childhood, which began in the chilly alps of

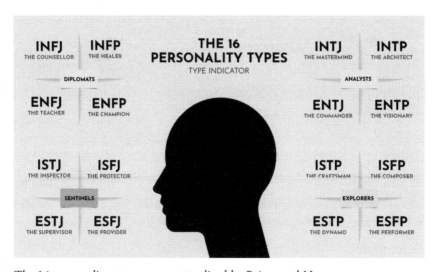

The 16 personality types as conceptualized by Briggs and Myers.

Switzerland, during the middle of summer. The clock read 7:27 pm in Kesswil, on Lake Constance. After three previous miscarriages for his mother, Emilie, Jung was the first surviving baby, which made him the eldest sibling. The sun – and Jung's consciousness – had just begun to rise.

CHAPTER 2

CHILDHOOD

During Jung's stage of Childhood, specific psychological phenomena unfold, shaping an individual's psyche. The development of the persona, an external façade presented to the world, begins to take shape as children learn to adapt to social expectations. Archetypal symbols, deeply embedded in myths and fairy tales, influence the child's imagination, contributing to the formation of early fantasies and dreams.

Moreover, the emergence of early memories, often laden with symbolic significance, becomes a focal point for understanding the unconscious dynamics at play. Jung highlights the role of parental figures and their archetypal representations, shaping the child's perception of authority and relationships. These experiences in childhood set the stage for the ongoing process of individuation, influencing an individual's journey towards self-discovery and integration.

ISSUES WITH PARENTS

Carl Jung was born on Monday, 26 July 1875 to a pastor of the Swiss Reformed Church (Paul Jung) and philologist (Emilie Preiswerk) in Kesswil, Switzerland. He had a highly religious upbringing with parents who had a tumultuous marriage. They fought often and with charged arguments over their children's upbringing and education.

He often spent free time alone and absorbed in his own projects, and saw little value in cultivating friendships. When he was four, his family moved to Basel, where he spent his primary education days in a local village school in Klein-Huningen. He was absorbed in creating his own fantasy worlds, complete with his own systems. The 'real', tangible world was absurd to little Jung.

His mother, who suffered from severe mental health issues, would often lock herself in a room in an attempt to communicate with spirits. Jung had a sense of *folie a deux* (that is, when symptoms from one person are transmitted to another) where he believed to have suffered from split personality disorder. Emilie kept little Jung on edge, because he was always walking on eggshells in her presence. Like mother ... like son?

He developed a fear of schizophrenia in himself from his mother's chronic dissociation, paranoia and neuroticism. To top it off, Jung believed she favoured his siblings over him, as she was often emotionally distant with him. When Jung's father passed away, she simply remarked, almost indifferently, 'He died in time for you.'

Jung focused on understanding the mother archetype after his father's passing. He associated many outward and magical connotations with the feminine archetypes and recognized both the light and dark sides of them. As one of the (usually first and) most important role models in a child's life, the mother helps lay the ground for their development and growth.

*Evil symbols are the witch, the dragon (or any devouring
and entwining animal, such as a large fish or a serpent),*

the grave, the sarcophagus, deep water, death, nightmares and bogies (Empusa, Lilith, etc.).

The qualities associated with it are maternal solicitude and sympathy; the magic authority of the female; the wisdom and spiritual exaltation that transcend reason; any helpful instinct or impulse; all that is benign, all that cherishes and sustains, that fosters growth and fertility.

On the negative side, the mother archetype may connote anything secret, hidden, dark; the abyss, the world of the dead, anything that devours, seduces and poisons, that is terrifying and inescapable like fate.

Kesswil, Jung's birth town in Switzerland.

Through his intricate notes, Jung mentioned that his mother would become extremely strange and mysterious – quietly on edge, so to speak – at night. One night, he claimed to have seen a faintly luminous and indefinite figure coming from her room, with a head detached from the neck and floating in the air in front of the body. A ghost or spirit of some sort, enough to etch a permanent mark in Jung's mind.

It was a terrifying and ghastly sight that would inspire many horror films, indeed. These countless supernatural encounters inspired Jung to delve deeper into the occult, when he matured and explored the depths of his psyche. Jung sought to integrate these diverse and esoteric perspectives from the occult into his psychological framework, bridging the gap between spirituality and psychology.

He later practised active imagination, a technique that involved engaging with the contents of his unconscious through visualization and dialogue. During these sessions, he would often encounter mystical or occult figures, such as Philemon, a wise old man, who became a central figure in his inner exploration and part of his archetypal structures for the collective unconscious.

In 1878, his parents separated briefly as Emilie went to a psychiatric hospital. At the age of three, Jung developed eczema and was cared for by his aunt, who was a devoutly religious nurse. According to his memoir, *Memories, Dreams, Reflections*, Jung described his aunt as a stern but loving caregiver who played an important role in his development. She encouraged his interest in nature and also introduced him to religion and spirituality.

From that point onwards, Jung was afraid he would associate womanly figures with unreliableness and instability. When he needed comfort, he was unable to find it consistently. By the age of seven, he had choking fits in his dreams, and nightmares about suffocation – with a dark, ominous figure chasing him. He also experienced night terrors, where he'd wake up in the middle of the night with an unshakable sense of impending doom.

My parents' house was full of spirits ... I never had any playmates of my own age. I had to play alone or with children much older or much younger than myself.

As a child, I felt myself to be alone, and I am still, because I know things and must hint at things which others apparently know nothing of, and for the most part do not want to know.

Despite her extended absences, Emilie had a strong influence on her son's early development, fostering his creativity and encouraging his interest in the supernatural. Jung remained close to his mother throughout her life, even though he had trouble understanding her thoughts most of the time. He even built a tower for her on his property in Bollingen, Switzerland, as a place of refuge, creativity, reflection – where she could be close to him during her final years.

In 1883, his father Paul showed him the evening sky, which was lit up with the celestial effects of the eruption of the Krakatoa volcano. Little Jung, then at the age of eight, saw his father as a dependable, steady figure with comfort and predictability, and viewed their interactions in a positive light. He was inspired by his tireless work as a minister, and initially wanted to follow in his footsteps. Like father, like son?

However, the thought of pursuing religious ministry was predictably short-lived. Jung dismally announced that theology had alienated him from his father, whom he saw as hopelessly entrapped by the Church's dogmatic views. Paul Jung was also a deeply troubled man who struggled with his own personal demons, including alcoholism and depression. At one point, he was known to have lost his faith with the introduction of the Enlightenment era.

> [My father Paul] was not a theological genius, but he was an honest and good man, and his preaching bore the stamp of his own character.

> Although he was busy with his pastoral duties, my father always found time for me. We took long walks together, and he showed me how to observe and appreciate the natural world around me.

Paul Jung's study was located directly below Carl's childhood bedroom, so the two were often at odds. Young Carl would often hear his father pacing and talking to himself as he worked. Jung felt his father was too rigid and lacked imagination, while his father criticized his son's intellectual pursuits and interest in the occult, which he saw as unorthodox and potentially dangerous.

His father died early at the age of 54, 'without the help of God', Jung believed. He always thought his father's preachings on grace were stale and hollow. Jung initially theorized that he did not have a father complex, despite his difficult relationship with his father, because he believed that he had successfully 'individuated' from his father.

The Krakatoa eruption of 1883, which the little Jung watched with his father.

However, later in life, Jung revised his thinking on the father complex and acknowledged that it was a more complicated and nuanced phenomenon than he had initially believed. He recognized that even individuals who had successful relationships with their fathers could still have unresolved psychological issues related to their father figures. He described the influence of a father as far-reaching and profound.

> *The father is the natural adversary of the son, and the son is the natural adversary of the father. It is through the relationship between them that the son is initiated into the masculine world, and the father into the feminine.*

> *In men, a positive father-complex very often produces a certain credulity with regard to authority and a distinct willingness to bow down before all spiritual dogmas and values; while in women, it induces the liveliest spiritual aspirations and interests.*

A TURNING POINT AT SCHOOL

Jung's early schooling days were tumultuous. Aged 12, he was knocked down unconscious by a rock thrown by a boy with such force that he suffered from recurring fainting spells and would have to skip classes due to his condition. Eventually, he was medically diagnosed with epilepsy. Jung recalled, 'From that point on, I became a serious child.' He had an alternative persona whom he believed had lived 100 years earlier; a dignified, authoritative individual.

This persona had 'no definable character at all – born, living, dead, everything in one, a total vision of life', according to Jung. This led his peers to give him the nickname 'Father Abraham'. He kept to himself mostly, for he was considered strange and aloof by his classmates. He was disturbed and had to conquer his own confusing thoughts that would test his patience and sanity, before he was even an adolescent!

A psychoneurosis must be understood, ultimately, as the suffering of a soul which has not discovered its meaning.

Neurosis is really an attempt at self-cure ... It is an attempt of the self-regulating psychic system to restore the balance, in no way different from the function of dreams – only rather more forceful and drastic.

Although Jung was outwardly quiet, he had a whole imaginary world buzzing inside his mind. He used the sharp edge of a wooden ruler to carve into a mannequin, which he hid inside a pencil case with a painted stone. With his own secret language, he'd communicate to the mannequin through slips of paper, and open a case that contained his 'ceremonial' objects. This process, Jung later figured out, was akin to rituals and totems in other cultures.

Jung attended the Humanistisches Gymnasium in Basel, Switzerland, for his formal education. The gymnasium provided a classical education in Latin and Greek, which would have exposed Jung to classical literature and philosophy. This classical education also influenced his later thinking and writing. Throughout his

A portrait of Carl Jung in elementary school.

schooling, he remained a solitary, detached and independent autodidact.

The stage of Childhood, encompassed with Jung's theory of individuation, underscores the pivotal role of early experiences in shaping an individual's psyche. He emphasizes the significance of archetypal symbols and the formation of the persona. Childhood essentially lays the foundation for one's journey towards self-discovery and integration. The child's fabric of reality is interwoven by the collective unconscious and its archetypes.

CHAPTER 3

YOUTH

What did you do as a child that made the hours pass like minutes? Herein lies the key to your earthly pursuits.

The stage of Youth constitutes a dynamic phase in Jung's psychological framework, and explores the intricate interplay between identity and the influence of deep-seated archetypes. Youth entails the emergence of a blurry self-image, an intensification of social interactions, and amplification of archetypal themes within the psyche. As individuals navigate the (often opposing) forces of societal and personal expectations, Jung's insights shed light on the archetypal patterns that highlight the wonders of Youth.

Jung's maturation from puberty to adulthood was a thoroughly challenging one. Since his interests were so diverse – from alchemy to Eastern religion – he struggled to select a single vocation. His mind was constantly on the lookout for new ideas to fully make sense of the world around him. Everything was interconnected but hieroglyphic, and he wanted (more than anything else) to understand why.

AN INTEREST IN SÉANCES

In his youth, Jung developed a keen interest in the captivating spectacle of séances. In 1896, he eagerly witnessed his cousin, Hélène Preiswerk, in a trance state, where she spoke in different voices and recounted tales from past lives. These entities spoke through her, often conveying messages, insights or knowledge that seemed to originate from beyond her conscious awareness.

In a letter addressed to J.B. Rhine, Jung refers to a young woman known as Hélène, highlighting her notable mediumistic abilities. Jung had encountered Hélène around the time of this peculiar event. In his autobiographical work, *Memories, Dreams, Reflections*, Jung mentions his involvement in a series of séances with his relatives.

However, it's important to note that these séances had been ongoing for some time before these incidents, with Hélène playing a central role. Interestingly, Jung already had a close relationship with Hélène, who, by all accounts, harboured romantic feelings for him. This situation hints at Jung's early, somewhat ambiguous engagement with the occult.

During these séances, Hélène would enter a trance-like state, collapsing to the floor and speaking in the voice of a man named Samuel Preiswerk, even though she had never heard him. She conveyed messages, urging the participants to pray for her elder sister, Bertha, claiming that Bertha had given birth to a child with African heritage. Coincidentally, Bertha, residing in Brazil, had previously given birth to a child and delivered another child on the same day as the séance.

Subsequent séances continued to yield remarkable outcomes. Notably, Samuel Preiswerk and Jung's grandfather, Karl, who had a

Hélène Preiswerk, Jung's cousin who experienced séances.

strained relationship in life, apparently reconciled in the spirit world. There were also ominous warnings, such as a prediction of the loss of an unborn child for another sister, which tragically occurred when the baby was born prematurely and deceased in August.

Among the various voices Hélène channelled, the most intriguing was that of a spirit named Ivenes, who claimed to be the genuine Hélène Preiswerk. This persona exhibited greater maturity, confidence and intelligence compared to the absent-minded, seemingly less bright, talented or educated Hélène.

It appeared as if a more robust personality, similar to Jung's concept of the 'Other', lay hidden beneath the surface of the unremarkable teenager. This insight into the human psyche would later influence Jung's theory of 'individuation', the process of becoming one's true self. Hélène did eventually flourish, achieving success as a dressmaker in France, though her life was tragically cut short at the age of 30.

DREAMS AND ACADEMIA

Unfortunately, Jung had no money to study anywhere except for Basel, which did not have an option to study archaeology. His financial situation left him devastated and disappointed since he felt like his choices were far too limited. He kept postponing the decision to select a field of study, which concerned his father.

To Jung's surprise, he had two vivid dreams that involved vastly different roads, which he had recounted in great detail:

In the first dream I was in a dark wood that stretched along the Rhine. I came to a little hill, a burial mound, and began to dig. After a while I turned up, to my astonishment, some bones of prehistoric animals.

This interested me enormously, and at that moment I knew: I must get to know nature, the world in which we live, and the things around us.

Then came a second dream.

Again I was in a wood; it was threaded with watercourses, and in the darkest place I saw a circular pool, surrounded by dense undergrowth.

Half immersed in the water laid the strangest and most wonderful creature: a round animal, shimmering in opalescent hues ... this magnificent creature should be lying there undisturbed, in the hidden place ... it aroused in me an intense desire for knowledge, so that I awoke with a beating heart.

And so, Jung went along with his dreams to pursue medicine academically over archaeology. He wondered why people had to settle for one career, for there was a grand buffet of knowledge to be uncovered. And so began his dive head-first in the rabbit hole of Eastern religions, art and anthropology. He began his post-secondary studies in medicine at the University of Basel.

Jung felt that medical studies were necessary for him to gain a solid scientific foundation and to pursue his interests in psychiatry and psychology. However, he found some aspects of the medical

The University of Basel, where Jung studied medicine.

curriculum to be limiting, particularly in terms of its emphasis on pathology and the physical aspects of illness.

He worked tenaciously under the famous neurologist Richard von Krafft-Ebing, to whom he connected the dots inside his mind between psychology and medical sciences. This 'a-ha!' moment came to him during the last day of his studies in medicine, prior to his final exam. Jung read Krafft-Ebing's brief introduction to his book of psychiatry – and his perspectives changed there.

During this time, he also devoured philosophical texts on Nietzsche, Kant, Schopenhauer, Haeckel, Swedenborg and Eduard von Hartmann. These authors, among others, played a role in shaping Jung's intellectual foundation and the development of his own theories and concepts in psychology and analytical psychology. If Jung was a student today, he may have qualified for a double major (or at least a minor) in philosophy!

Philosophy, at its core, is a quest for wisdom; a search for truth that encompasses both rational thinking and intuitive insights.

Philosophy should not be confined to academic discourse; it should be a living, personal exploration that connects us to the larger questions of existence.

Jung's dissatisfaction with the medical education system at the time is evident in his correspondence and writings. He expressed frustration with the reductionist tendencies of medical training and sought to explore areas beyond the scope of conventional medicine. Jung suggested that a holistic approach – considering the interplay of mind, body and spirit – was necessary for a comprehensive understanding of human health.

Jung began to interpret dreams professionally in the late 1890s, around 1897 or 1898, while he was still a medical student. His early experiences with dream interpretation were primarily focused on his own dreams. He began keeping a dream journal in his early twenties, and became increasingly interested in the symbolic language of dreams and their connection to the unconscious. The rest is history.

One of Jung's most significant early internal experiences was a recurring dream he had as a child. In the dream, he would see a large stone phallus, which he interpreted as a symbol of the power of the unconscious. He later realized that the phallus was also a symbol of the divine creative force, which he would later explore in his theories on the collective unconscious.

Phallic symbols are often linked to concepts of vitality and strength. Jung's dream may be reflecting a sense of personal empowerment, a large pool of untapped creative energy, or a need to tap into his inner reservoirs of strength. It can also represent masculine energy; the itch to take action, think decisively, and take meticulous action in order to achieve goals.

As a medical student still undergoing his studies, Jung also had a dream in which he saw a dark underground chamber, which he interpreted as a symbol of the unconscious. He saw himself exploring the chamber and discovering ancient artefacts and relics, which he interpreted as symbols of the collective unconscious and the shared cultural heritage of humanity. During his studies, Jung still made time to read books outside of medicine for leisure.

Afterwards, he studied psychology at the University of Zurich.

Carl Jung at the Burghölzli Psychiatric Clinic, where he worked, c.1910.

When he picked up a textbook on psychiatry, his fascination was fuelled by curiosity. This inspired him to undergo an internship at the Burghölzli Psychiatric Clinic from 1900 to 1909. As the field of psychiatry was considered one of the least respected branches in medicine at the time, Jung was taking a professional risk. However, he followed his intuition and hunger for understanding.

JUNG'S COLLABORATIONS WITH JANET

In the winter of 1902–03, Jung studied with Pierre Janet, a French psychologist and philosopher, in Paris. In 1905, Jung was promoted to senior physician at the clinic, as well as lecturer of psychiatry at the University of Zurich. Janet had developed a method of studying the mental processes of individuals with hysteria and other neuroses, and Jung was interested in learning more about this approach.

Janet was a lecturer at College de France at the time. While Jung was studying alongside his fellow psychologist, he explored many museums around the country, the most notable one being the Louvre. He dedicated special focus to ancient art, including Egyptian artefacts and the masterpieces of the Renaissance era by artists such as Fra Angelico, Leonardo da Vinci, Rubens and Frans Hals.

Jung acquired paintings and engravings, even having some paintings replicated for decorating his new residence. His artistic pursuits spanned both oil and watercolour mediums. In January 1903, he journeyed to London, where he extensively explored the collections at its museums, with a particular emphasis on the Egyptian, Aztec and Inca exhibits within the British Museum.

Upon returning, he assumed a vacant position at the Burghölzli and concentrated his research efforts on the analysis of linguistic

Pierre Janet.

associations, collaborating with Franz Riklin in this endeavour. The groundwork for Jung's early work can be accredited to the likes of Théodore Flournoy and Janet, two scientists he admired greatly and was eager to work with.

However, despite their initial collaboration, Jung and Janet eventually developed different ideas about the nature of the psyche and the best methods for treating mental illness. Janet focused on the study of dissociation and the importance of early childhood experiences, while Jung emphasized the role of the unconscious and the need for individuals to explore their own inner worlds in order to achieve psychological growth and healing.

STRIKING OUT ON HIS OWN

By 1916, he founded the Psychological Club of Zurich to popularize the growing field of psychiatry. His experience with his own patients led him to publish *On the Psychology and Pathology of So-Called Occult Phenomena,* which focuses on the grey area between epilepsy and hysteria.

Jung approached occult phenomena from a psychological perspective, seeking to understand them as products of the human mind rather than accepting them as purely supernatural or paranormal. He was interested in the subjective experiences and perceptions of individuals who reported such phenomena.

He introduced the concept of archetypes in this essay. He suggested that the symbols, images and experiences associated with occult phenomena may be expressions of universal archetypal patterns that are present in the collective unconscious of humanity. These archetypal elements can shape the way individuals interpret and experience occult events.

Jung also explored the potential pathological aspects of occult experiences. He acknowledged that some individuals who claim to have encountered occult phenomena may be suffering from psychological disorders or disturbances. Jung was also deeply interested in distinguishing between genuine mystical experiences and those that were the result of mental illness.

He emphasized the importance of symbolism in understanding occult phenomena, and argues that many occult experiences involve symbolic imagery. These symbols can provide insights into the unconscious mind of the individual. In essence, deciphering the symbolism could lead to a better understanding of the underlying psychological processes.

Jung discussed the role of altered states of consciousness in occult experiences. He suggested that altered states, such as trance or heightened emotional states, can play a significant role in the perception of occult phenomena and the emergence of archetypal imagery – the intersection between the supernatural and active imagination.

Overall, Jung's essay *On the Psychology and Pathology of So-Called Occult Phenomena* reflects his early interest in the intersection of psychology, mythology and the supernatural. It laid the groundwork for his later work on analytical psychology and the exploration of the deep, permeable layers of the human psyche.

Jung's involvement with the club allowed him to collaborate with other influential figures in the field, including Eugen Bleuler, J.B. Rhine and Karl Abraham – among others. He used the club's platform to present some of his most prestigious works, such as *The Structure of the Unconscious*, which present a deeper dive into the collective unconscious and archetypes.

Eugen Bleuler was the director of the Burghölzli clinic and he was a great influence on Jung.

STUDIES AND EXPERIMENTS

Jung also published *Studies in Word Association* in 1906, which outlines the experiments Jung had conducted at the University of Zurich pertaining to various psychopathological conditions. His own wife – the then Jungian analyst pioneer Emma Jung – was one of the first participants in the study.

In the comprehensive series of studies, Jung conducted experiments in which he presented individuals with a list of words and asked them to respond with the first word that came to their minds when presented with each word. These word association tests aimed to explore the spontaneous and unfiltered responses of participants.

The Word Association Experiment involves presenting a list of one hundred words and requesting immediate associations from the participant. The experimenter monitors response times using a stopwatch. This process is then repeated, and any statistically divergent responses are noted.

Subsequently, the participant is invited to provide feedback on words that prompted longer-than-average response times, purely mechanical reactions, or altered associations during the second iteration. These instances, termed 'complex indicators' by the facilitator, are then subject to discussion with the participant.

The outcome is akin to a detailed 'map' of individual emotional complexes, serving as a valuable tool for enhancing self-awareness and identifying common sources of turmoil that often plague relationships. What transpires during the association test mirrors what frequently occurs in interpersonal conversations.

The exchange loses its impartial nature and its underlying goals, as the activated complexes interfere with the communicator's intentions, potentially leading them to express ideas they later struggle to recall. These lapses in short-term memory can lead to clues of what had been rooted in the long-term Pandora's box of incredibly salient yet repressed long-term, life-altering experiences.

Jung used the results of these word association tests to study what he called 'complexes'. Complexes are emotionally charged clusters of thoughts, feelings and memories that are often outside of conscious awareness. Jung believed that word associations could reveal the presence of complexes and help to uncover unconscious material.

Jung paid close attention to the emotional content of the word associations. He believed that *strong* emotional reactions to certain words could indicate the presence of underlying psychological conflicts. For example, associating the word 'marriage' with positive terms such as 'long-lasting' and 'peaceful' over a negative term like 'quarrelsome' can hint at underlying, potentially unresolved issues hidden deep in someone's psyche.

Through his research, he introduced the idea of repression, where certain thoughts or feelings are pushed into the unconscious because they are unacceptable or painful. He also examined resistance, which refers to the reluctance or inability of an individual to express or acknowledge certain thoughts or emotions.

Studies in Word Association represents a pivotal point in Jung's early research, marking the genesis of several foundational concepts in psychology. Through word association tests, Jung delved into the intricate realm of the unconscious, uncovering emotional complexes, resistance and repressed content that significantly influenced an individual's mental landscape.

This work also illuminated the distinction between the personal and collective unconscious, laying the groundwork for his later exploration of archetypes and the universal symbols embedded in the human psyche. By scrutinizing the spontaneous responses to words, Jung unveiled the intricate tapestry of the human mind, bridging the gap between conscious and unconscious processes.

These early investigations in *Studies in Word Association* paved the way for the development of analytical psychology and shaped Jung's enduring contributions to the field of psychology, ultimately influencing the understanding of the complexity of human consciousness and the towering impact of linguistics on emotions and expressions.

EMMA JUNG ENTERS THE PICTURE

Jung met Emma Rauschenbach when she was still a schoolgirl in 1896 through his mother, and simply 'knew' she would become his wife one day. His intuition spoke to him of their long-lasting relationship that would transcend the normal constraints of what would be deemed as socially acceptable.

Jung crossed paths with Emma again when he was a young man. He was working as a psychiatric assistant at the Burghölzli hospital in Zurich, and she was the sister of one of his patients. Jung and Emma were attracted to each other when they both became adults, and immediately formed a close bond. Their personalities complemented each other, and they shared interests in art, literature and philosophy.

After their initial meeting, Jung and Emma exchanged letters over a period of time. These letters revealed a deep emotional connection and intellectual rapport. Jung often attributed his sense of destiny in marrying Emma to his dreams and intuition. He described having dreams and inner experiences that suggested their connection was significant and fated.

To any onlooker, his proposal seemed outrageous. She was a wealthy, well-educated Swiss heiress, whereas he was then a poor, unknown psychiatrist with a slightly unkempt appearance. Olden day *Titanic*, if you will ... did the hearts of both go on? It appeared to be so – seven years later, they were married on 14 February 1903.

The pair met through a mutual acquaintance, Otto Gross, who was a patient of Jung's, and later became a colleague. While Gross was attending psychiatric sessions with Jung, he developed a friendship with Emma's brother, Ernst Bernhard Rauschenbach.

Carl Jung with his wife, Emma.

Their shared interest in the burgeoning field of psychiatry brought them all together.

And so began one of the most under told and wildest love stories of two incredibly complex individuals – Carl and Emma Jung.

THE LARGELY UNTOLD STORY OF MISS SPIELREIN – A DIVE INTO TRANSFERENCE?

Jung worked closely with a hysteric Russian Jewish patient named Sabina Spielrein, whom he first met in 1904 at the Burghölzli psychiatric hospital. Later on, after many sessions together, she became his experimental assistant and rumoured love interest. She had also written numerous letters to Sigmund Freud, and challenged his rigorous beliefs on the birth and death instinct.

It's plausible that Jung may have garnered a great deal of inspiration for his concept of the *anima* (the unconscious feminine side of men's psyches), and its counterpart, the *animus* (the unconscious masculine side of women's psyches) from Sabina. They were involved with each other, intertwined with passion and shared research interests. Even though it was legally frowned upon to engage in extramarital affairs, Jung was presented with a conundrum. Should he leave his wife to spend the rest of his life with this new woman he was heads over heels in love with? In the end, Jung decided to have his cake and eat it too.

In 1907, at the end of his Youth, Jung met with Freud for the first time in Vienna. The pair reportedly spoke for over half a day during their first conversation on the human psyche and hit it off immediately. The famous Jung–Freud letters depicted the deterioration of their relationship as their views on the profession were grossly mismatched. Freud was stubborn in his rigid empirical explanations, whereas Jung saw value in a subjective approach.

After meeting Jung, Sabina also developed a close professional relationship with Freud through exchanging letters, which began in 1909. She saw Freud as a father figure, with whom she could talk freely about her perplexing and complicated feelings for her psychiatrist, Jung. He noted her bright ideas for the field of psychoanalysis and supported her career through every stage and new discovery.

Sabina sheepishly admitted to Freud, 'I was very much ashamed of myself, of my being in love with Jung, and I was ashamed of my being ashamed of myself. You know what a bad opinion I have of myself. But now, as the emotional chaos subsides, I see more clearly, and I am not ashamed any more.' (30 September 1909.)

The Spielrein family, with Sabina second from left, c.1909.

The energy from her internal turmoil may have inspired her to get to the bottom of what the anima consists of.

In another one of Sabina's letters to Freud, she wrote, 'I know now that my passion for Jung was my desire to be united with my father, but it was also my desire for self-affirmation, my desire to be a person in my own right, to be able to stand on my own two feet. Now I understand that I cannot live without psychoanalysis.' (12 November 1909.)

During their rather controversial relationship, Jung wrote many case studies on Sabina, even though he went far beyond the traditional boundaries of doctor–patient interactions. The movie *A Dangerous Method* starring Michael Fassbender and Keira Knightley visually illustrates what may have happened during this confusing period – a process known as *transference.*

Transference is a psychoanalytic term that describes the patient's unconscious redirection of their feelings and desires from one person to another, usually towards the therapist. (However, it may also occur the other way around.) In the case of transference, the patient develops romantic or sexual feelings towards their therapist, which can be complex and emotionally charged.

Sabina wrote to Jung, with no holds barred, 'I feel that you are the only person in the world who understands me, who can help me, who can lead me out of the darkness and into the light,' (6 February 1909), and a few months later, 'I am glad that you are my doctor and my friend. You have given me a new life, and I am forever grateful to you.' (7 July 1909.)

Jung wrote back, 'Your last letter made me very happy. It is a great joy to me to be able to help you and to see you making progress in your analysis. You are one of my most interesting patients, and

I feel a special connection with you.' (22 December 1909.) Their chemistry and compatibility helped strengthen their professional relationship, even though it was (and still is) considered taboo.

In his writings about Spielrein, Jung acknowledged her intelligence, sensitivity and insight. He called her 'remarkable' and 'gifted' and believed she possessed a deep understanding of the workings of the psyche. He believed that she had a natural talent for psychoanalysis, and that she had the potential to become a great psychologist in her own right (clairvoyant – he was correct!). Sabina went on to become one of the world's first female psychoanalysts.

A few years later, after many sessions of deep emotional and intellectual connection with Sabina, Jung wrote, 'I am very impressed by your courage and your determination to confront your deepest fears and desires. You have a strong will and a resilient spirit, and I believe that these qualities will serve you well in the future.' (2 January 1911.) Sabina married Russian Jewish physician Pavel Sheftel in 1912 and moved to Berlin to continue her professional career.

In 1910, Jung also became the chief editor for the *Yearbook for Psychoanalytical and Psychopathological Research* and the president of the International Psychoanalytical Association. Around this time, he began to write *Psychology of the Unconscious*. The book redefines libido as fluid psychic energy, and compares directed thinking and dreams. Less Freudian explanations, more Jungian mystique.

MISS WOLFF, ANOTHER POTENTIAL SUITRESS?

In 1910, Jung met Toni Wolff, another patient at the Burghölzli psychiatric hospital. Their relationship was initially professional.

Over time, it became increasingly complex and intertwined – as Jung developed an attraction towards Toni that was reciprocated. Despite these complications, they continued to work together on the development of the anima, as well as the study of alchemy and symbolism.

Jung and Toni spent a great deal of time in the Bollingen Tower, a personal retreat house he built in the 1920s. He referred to her as his 'second wife', who helped him understand the complexities of the anima, which caused immense tension in his marriage to his spouse Emma. Toni was in a long-term relationship with another man at the time, which further complicated their mutually polyamorous situation.

From 1925 to 1928, she became a key figure in Jung's life, and contributed to his work. She had a profound influence on the formation of the anima and animus. When 1928 hit, Jung experienced a personal crisis, and Toni provided support during this challenging period. However, in 1944 Toni Wolff moved out of his household.

The continued marital strain between Jung and his wife was exacerbated by his involvement with multiple other women, most of them being his clients. This caused a constant stream of tension in their family life and relational dynamics. Jung had little time for his children, as he spent most of his time deeply absorbed in his work and research.

Miss Wolff, at that point, was an accomplished psychoanalyst in her own right, and moving out was the natural next step towards asserting professional independence in the field of psychiatry. She likely ventured out to establish her own office and make a mark in the world, and never married as her professional work was of the utmost importance.

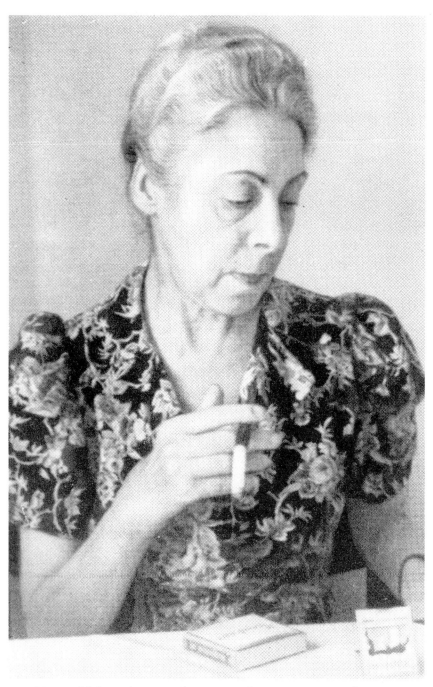

Miss Toni Wolff, latter-day research partner and romantic interest of Jung.

'I shall always be grateful to Toni for doing for my husband what I or anyone else could not have done at a most critical time,' remarked Emma Jung.

Toni commented on Emma as well, in C.G. *Jung, Emma Jung and Toni Wolff – A Collection of Remembrances*:

'You know, sometimes if a man's wife is big enough to leap over the hurdle of self-pity, she may find that her supposed rival has even helped her marriage! His "other woman" [Toni herself] can sometimes help a man live out certain aspects of himself that his wife either can't fulfil, or else doesn't especially want to. As a result, some of the wife's energies are now freed for her own creative interests and development, often with the result that the marriage not only survives, but emerges even stronger than before!'

Jung wrote a long-winded letter to his colleague, James, around the time of Toni's premature death in 1953 as he needed to process his emotions by letting them out through words.

Toni Wolff's death was so sudden, so totally unexpected, that one could hardly realize her passing. I had seen her only two days before.

The Hades dreams I had in the middle of February I related entirely to myself because nothing pointed to Toni Wolff.

At the beginning of my illness in Oct. 52 I dreamt of a huge black elephant that uprooted a tree. The uprooting of a tree can signify death.

Since then I have dreamt several times of elephants which I always had to treat warily. Apparently they were engaged in road-building.

Jung's stage of Youth serves as a significant juncture in his psychological framework, marked by the intensification of personal and social dynamics. The challenges of forging one's identity amid societal pressures and interpersonal relationships define this stage. All these efforts contribute to the individuation process, whereby an individual swims through the murky waters of developing an identity, which brings upon the next stage...

CHAPTER 4

MIDDLE LIFE

The stage of Middle Life is faced with the complexities of adults navigating the demands of their career, relationships and societal expectations. The infamous 'midlife crisis' arises from the subconscious at this point, where individuals may realize they still have time, yet have already gone through half of their life. They may grapple with the reconciliation of earlier life choices and pursue a deeper meaning. Perhaps they may start dressing differently and change their career, and drop everything on a whim.

The strife between Freud and Jung marked his challenging passage into Middle Life, around the early 1910s. Jung would spend days without an appetite and mourning the loss of an academic relationship with someone he respected and looked up to academically. His thoughts spiralled day in and day out. Why did Freud decide to cut off communication altogether? Surely there could have been a way to keep in touch? The Jung–Freud feud is a compelling chapter in the history of psychology, characterized by the eventual divergence of two influential figures in the field, and marked a turning point in Jung's career.

FREUD AND JUNG'S LONG-WINDED, CHALLENGING RELATIONSHIP

Sigmund Freud and Carl Jung had a close and collaborative relationship for several years before their eventual split. Jung initially admired Freud and his work, and their collaboration began around 1906. Jung was drawn to Freud's theories on the unconscious mind and the significance of dreams, and he saw Freud as a mentor and father figure. Their initial collaboration was marked by mutual admiration, with Jung becoming a leading figure in the psychoanalytic movement after their first meeting in 1907. He even assumed the role of president of the International Psychoanalytical Association in 1910.

Freud, Jung and other psychologists at Clark University, 1909.

However, over time, philosophical and theoretical differences emerged between them. One major point of contention was the emphasis Freud placed on sexuality as a primary driving force in human behaviour. Jung began to develop his own theories, expanding on the concept of the unconscious and incorporating elements of mythology, religion and spirituality.

The relationship between Freud and Jung began to deteriorate in the early 1910s as their differences became more pronounced. Jung's growing interest in spirituality and mysticism, as well as his divergence from Freudian psychoanalysis, led to increasing tensions. The final straw was Jung's publication of his book *Symbols of Transformation* in 1912, which presented ideas that were completely inconsistent with Freud's views.

However, the crux of their conflict lay in their differing theoretical perspectives, particularly on the nature of the unconscious and libido. While Jung initially expanded on Freud's ideas, he eventually introduced his own concepts, such as the collective unconscious, archetypes and a broader consideration of spirituality in the human psyche.

Sigmund was a thorough sceptic, dismissing occult phenomena as a 'black tide of mud'. However, during their heated discussion in Vienna concerning the supernatural in 1909, Jung felt a sudden warmth in his diaphragm. Abruptly, a bookcase in the room emitted a loud crack, startling them both.

Jung seized the moment, attributing it to a 'catalytic exteriorization phenomenon' in line with his belief that the eerie occurrences might be projections of internal conflicts. Freud dismissed it as nonsense, but Jung confidently predicted another crack, which promptly occurred.

Regarding the Oedipus complex (a child's possessive sexual desires for their opposite-sex parent), Jung eventually concluded that the connection between a child and its mother didn't arise from underlying incestuous desires. Instead, he believed it originated from the mother being the primary source of love and care for the child.

With great sadness from Jung, their relationship ultimately collapsed in 1913, and he resigned from his position as the president of the International Psychoanalytical Association. This marked the end of their professional collaboration and friendship but both men continued to make significant contributions to the field of psychology, each developing his own school of thought.

Despite the animosity, both Jung and Freud attempted reconciliation later in their lives, but their relationship never fully recovered. The Jung–Freud feud remains significant in the history of psychology, representing a major schism between two influential thinkers, each of whom played a pivotal role in shaping the development of psychoanalytic and psychological theories.

Jung knew his order of operations in psychiatry sported a more theoretical and inductive slant rather than Freud's cut-and-dried empirical approach. Jung's emotional turmoil from 1913 can be attributed to two factors. Firstly, the relationship between Jung and Freud was not merely professional; Jung deeply respected and looked up to Freud as a mentor and father figure in the field of psychology. The rupture in their connection likely triggered a sense of loss, disappointment and abandonment for Jung. Moreover, the intellectual and emotional investment he had made in his work with Freud added to the weight of this separation. Jung's passion for his ideas and his desire for collaboration and validation from someone he admired left him grappling with feelings of isolation and self-doubt.

The decision to cut off communication was not made lightly by either Jung or Freud. It was, in many ways, a response to the irreconcilable differences in their theories and the intense emotional strain that the conflict had placed on their relationship. For Jung, the need to explore and develop his own theories and concepts was paramount, and he felt that maintaining a close connection with Freud might hinder this process.

While in hindsight, it might seem that they could have found a way to keep in touch, the emotional intensity of their disagreements and the desire to preserve their respective ideas and legacies likely made such a reconciliation extremely challenging. The separation, while painful for Jung, ultimately allowed him to embark on a transformative journey of self-discovery and the development of his own unique contributions to psychology. Jung wrote to Freud in 1913:

Dear Professor Freud,

I regret that our recent discussions have been marked by such tension and disagreement. I believe that we both have valuable contributions to make to the field of psychoanalysis, and I hope that we can find a way to work together more effectively in the future.

I must confess that I am disappointed by your recent criticisms of my work. I believe that my research has the potential to significantly advance the field of psychoanalysis, and I hope that you will take a more positive view of my contributions in the future.

Sigmund Freud, father of psychoanalysis.

I am writing to inform you that I have decided to discontinue my membership in the International Psychoanalytic Association. I believe that the organization has become too focused on promoting your own ideas at the expense of the broader field of psychoanalysis, and I no longer feel that it is an appropriate forum for my own research and interests.

Unfortunately, to Jung's dismay, Freud ended their friendship abruptly soon after, with a rather blunt and emotionally jarring letter:

Your allegation that I treat my followers as patients is demonstrably untrue … it is a convention among us analysts that none of us need feel ashamed of his own neurosis.

But one [meaning Jung] who while behaving abnormally keeps shouting that he is normal gives ground for the suspicion that he lacks insight into his illness.

Accordingly, I propose that we abandon our personal relations entirely.

In a letter to Freud later in 1913, Jung wrote, 'I accede to your wish that we abandon our personal relations, for I never thrust my friendship on anyone. You yourself are the best judge of what this moment means to you. The rest is silence.' In another letter after a few months of their separation, Jung wrote again to Freud: 'The break with you has been the greatest and most painful experience of my life.'

Jung also struggled with feelings of betrayal and abandonment, as he had invested so much of his time and energy into the psychoanalytic movement, only to be rejected by his former mentor and colleague. Now that his mentor and professor figure has left him, what is Jung to do? Trek bravely into the foggy woods of understanding alone? Find a new figure in the hope that they can guide him on a new journey?

The separation from Freud also resulted in a period of professional isolation for Jung. He felt somewhat ostracized from the psychoanalytic community at the time, as many of his colleagues remained loyal to Freud. Jung channelled his energy and emotions into his writing and research. He authored significant works during this period, including *Symbols of Transformation* (published in 1912), in which he began to outline his own ideas about the unconscious mind and the process of individuation.

After parting ways with Freud, Jung developed his own school of psychology known as *analytical psychology*. This marked a significant turning point in his career. He began to explore concepts like the collective unconscious, archetypes and individuation – which became the main course, the meat-and-potatoes of analytical psychology.

From personal fulfilment to the exploration of archetypes, individuation is considered one of the cornerstones of analytical psychology. Jung emphasized the importance of wholeness and integration within oneself. He noted how the integration of opposites – the balance between internal masculine and feminine forces – are integral to greater purpose and meaning.

A PIVOT INTO THE DEPTHS OF THE UNCONSCIOUS

Just a few months later, in 1913, Jung had a pivotal experience with intense turmoil – which he referred to as his 'confrontation with the unconscious' when he made his most significant trip to Italy. During this time, he had vivid visions and heard nightmarish voices that he believed were a grand manifestation of the collective unconscious during his deep depression and midlife crisis.

He saw an image of an immense and mysterious medieval cathedral, and knew right away that he had to confront it. Jung scurried back to his hotel room and detailed his racing thoughts. One of his dreams involved a series of underground chambers filled with ancient artefacts and symbols. These may have represented the hidden knowledge that Jung had yet to uncover.

In October, on a train to Schaffhausen, Jung dreamt of witnessing a flood that had submerged the majority of Europe, with the swirling yellow water turning into blood (a possible allusion to Revelations, the last chapter of the Bible?). Two weeks later, he experienced the same vision with more intensity, with a booming voice at the end of his dream that said to him, 'Look at it well, it is wholly real, and it will be so.'

He explored the rich history and architecture of Rome, Florence and Venice – but stumbled upon something marvellous in the small town of Ravenna. There, he had a vision that shook him to his core, as if he was 'sucked into a whirlpool of darkness'. This experience marked a turning point in his life and work, and he began to develop his ideas about archetypes, the collective unconscious, and the individuation process.

I was caught in a maelstrom, and the centre of it was a bubbling cauldron of frightening images. My soul was in chaos. I felt like I was going insane, and I was terrified that I would never be able to find my way back to sanity.

I saw a monstrous flood covering all the northern and low-lying lands between the North Sea and the Alps ... I saw yellow waves, swimming slime, and the stench of petroleum ... I saw a great city in flames, and a voice cried out in despair 'The City of Gold is destroyed!'

My whole being was so shaken that it was as if a thunderbolt had struck me. I was conscious of no objectivity or subjective judgement. I saw and heard things, neither heard nor seen by others.

Throughout his Middle Life, Jung heard strange voices all around him (similar to his mother when he was still a child). He dubbed this experience 'abaissement du niveau mental', which roughly translates to the lowering of one's consciousness. This process allows subconscious thoughts to more easily rise to the surface, which can be confusing – and even frightening. He feared, night after sleepless night, that he was losing touch with reality.

It was truly a period of intense psychological suffering that left him feeling disoriented, confused and even suicidal. At one point, Jung began to experience symptoms that he believed were similar to those of schizophrenia, including delusions and hallucinations. However, he also recognized that his experience was different from that of a typical schizophrenic, as he maintained a clear sense of self and was able to articulate his thoughts and feelings coherently.

During this time, he garnered an even greater interest in the paranormal and supernatural. He coined the term *synchronicity*, which loosely describes events that appear to be related at first glance but lack a logical connection. In other words, a highly meaningful coincidence. An example of this could be reappearing numbers, such as the famous 'angel number' 11:11 suggesting to someone that they should take the initiative in their life.

During this period, Jung was treating a young woman who possessed a high level of education and a serious demeanour. He recognized that her quest for psychological transformation faced

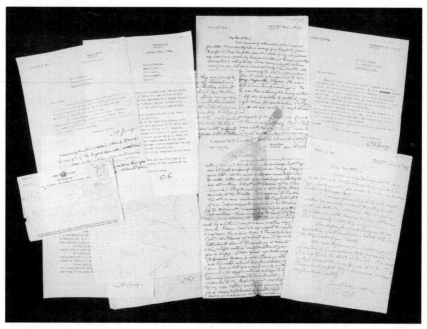

A collection of letters from Jung.

significant challenges, primarily due to her strong rationalist outlook. Jung understood that her path to change would remain difficult unless he could find a way to soften her rigid, rational shell with a touch of 'more human understanding'. He kept a watchful eye on the young woman, hopeful that something 'unexpected and irrational' might occur to aid in her transformation.

One day, as she recounted a dream from the previous night involving an expensive piece of jewellery resembling a golden scarab, a peculiar event transpired. While they were in the midst of their session, a tapping sound drew Jung's attention to the window. *Tap, tap.* To his surprise, he had to investigate what exactly was causing the ruckus.

Opening it, he reached out and plucked a scarab beetle, specifically a common rose-chafer (*Cetonia aurata*), out of the air. Jung remarked on the unusual behaviour of the beetle, which, contrary to its typical habits, had seemingly been compelled to enter the room at that very moment.

Remarkably, the beetle closely resembled the scarab from the woman's dream. It was the perfect synchronicity that Jung had been hoping for, and it held the potential to serve as a transformative catalyst for both the woman and her therapy. With a sense of revelation, Jung handed her the beetle and said, 'Here is your scarab,' creating a powerful connection between her dream imagery and the tangible external world.

This synchronistic event marked a profound moment in his own self-discovery, leading him to explore the symbolism of the scarab beetle and its relevance to his personal journey. This incident deepened Jung's understanding of the role of symbols in the unconscious and the interconnectedness of inner and outer experiences.

Synchronicity is the coming together of inner and outer events in a way that cannot be explained by cause and effect and that is meaningful to the observer.

Synchronicity can also be thought of as the occurrence of meaningful coincidences that cannot be explained by cause-and-effect relationships. According to Jung, synchronicity represents a connection between the inner and outer worlds, and suggests the presence of a deeper, underlying order or intelligence in the universe. An example of synchronicity could be thinking about an old friend and suddenly receiving a text from them that very instant, out of the blue.

Jung believed that synchronicity was closely related to the concept of the collective unconscious, which he saw as a shared reservoir of archetypes and psychic patterns that are common to all human beings. He suggested that synchronistic events occur when the unconscious contents of one person are resonant with the unconscious contents of another, resulting in a meaningful coincidence that cannot be explained in a conventional or logical way.

When we observe statistically, we eliminate the synchronicity phenomenon, and conversely, when we establish synchronicity, we must abandon the statistical method.

Another colourful example of synchronicity in Jung's journey is when he was struck with awe by a drawing that depicted a yogi with five human-like figures sprouting out from the top of his head; each of those heads with five *more* figures growing on top of those heads. Jung believed this drawing represented the many egos that the yogi was attempting to remove himself from to grow into the more holistic and objective state of the self.

A man who has not passed through the inferno of his passions has never overcome them. They then dwell in the house next door, and at any moment a flame may dart out and set fire to his own house.

Whenever we give up, leave behind, and forget too much, there is always the danger that the things we have neglected will return with added force.

A PSYCHOTIC BREAK

Through this 'psychotic break' as Jung called it, he proclaimed to be able to dive deeper into his unconscious mind – and continued to investigate. His book, *Memories, Dreams, Reflections* explains how he induced his hallucinations on command with active imagination. Jung also addressed how free will is connected to the abstraction of our thoughts. Most notably, it details his travels to Africa, India and Italy.

Jung's 'psychotic break' is often described as a crisis of his own psyche, during which he grappled with intense inner experiences and psychological turmoil. He saw this phase as a descent into his own unconscious, where he encountered a multitude of images, fantasies and emotions that were initially overwhelming. However, instead of pathologizing these experiences, Jung recognized their potential significance and chose to explore them further.

During this time, Jung went through a series of profound and highly symbolic inner experiences and visions, which he documented in his famous *Red Book*. He described encounters with various inner figures and archetypal images, which he believed were manifestations of the unconscious.

These experiences were often chaotic and tumultuous, and they pushed Jung to the brink of his psychological stability. Jung's encounters with these inner figures, which included characters like Philemon and Salome, were central to his later work on individuation and the development of personality.

Philemon

Philemon is a prominent figure in Jung's inner experiences, and he is often considered a wise and guiding figure. Jung describes Philemon as an old, bearded man with the horns of a bull, which was a common symbol of ancient wisdom and nature.

Philemon represents the archetype of the wise old man, a common figure in mythology and psychology. He is associated with wisdom, guidance and a deep understanding of the mysteries of life and the unconscious.

In Jung's encounters with Philemon, he engaged in meaningful and transformative conversations, receiving valuable insights and guidance from this inner figure. Philemon played a crucial role in helping Jung navigate his inner world and the intense experiences he was going through.

Salome

Salome is another significant figure in Jung's inner experiences, and she represents a more complex and enigmatic aspect of the unconscious.

A page from the Red Book *depicting the figure of Philemon.*

She's often associated with sensuality, seduction and danger. In Jung's encounters with her, she is described as a dark and seductive temptress, often dancing with veils or performing erotic and provocative dances.

Jung's interactions with Salome were more tumultuous and challenging than those with Philemon. She represented the darker and more chaotic aspects of the unconscious, and her presence symbolized the potential dangers and seductive lures of the psyche.

Jung's encounters with Salome illustrate the idea that the unconscious is not only a source of wisdom and guidance (as represented by figures like Philemon) but also a repository of powerful and potentially destructive forces that need to be integrated and understood.

Philemon and Salome are just two examples of the many archetypal figures and symbols that Jung encountered during his inner experiences. They highlight the richness and complexity of the unconscious mind and the need to engage with both its positive and negative aspects in the process of psychological growth and self-realization. Jung's exploration of these figures deeply influenced his theories of the collective unconscious and the individuation process.

It's important to note that Jung's experiences were deeply personal and subjective. They were not necessarily characterized by classic symptoms of psychosis or a loss of touch with reality in the way that we typically associate with psychotic disorders. Instead, Jung viewed these experiences as a confrontation with the deeper layers of the human psyche and a journey towards self-discovery and integration.

Active Imagination

During this period, Jung actively engaged in a process he later termed 'active imagination'. Active imagination involves deliberately and consciously interacting with the contents of the unconscious. Jung induced and explored his hallucinations through this technique.

He would enter a state of inner reflection, intentionally summoning and conversing with the various figures and symbols that emerged from his unconscious mind. This process allowed him to engage with his inner world and gain valuable insights into his own psyche.

There are roughly six stages of active imagination, through Jung's technique:

1. **Relaxation:** Jung would typically start by relaxing in a quiet and comfortable setting. This state of relaxation is important to create a receptive and open mindset.

2. **Concentration:** Jung would focus his attention on a particular image, symbol or emotion that intrigued him or appeared significant. This could be an image from a dream, a memory or a spontaneous mental image that came to mind.

3. **Amplification:** Jung would then attempt to amplify and explore this image or symbol in his mind. He might ask himself questions about it, such as its meaning, associations and the emotions it evoked.

4. **Engagement:** He actively engaged with the imagery or symbol. He might imagine having a conversation with a figure from his dream, interact with it, or explore the symbol in a creative way.

5. **Recording:** Jung often kept a journal to record his experiences during active imagination. This allowed him to track his progress, insights and any recurring themes or symbols.

6. **Iteration:** Jung would repeat this process regularly, allowing for a gradual deepening of the exploration and insight into his own psyche.

Active imagination can also be employed for problem-solving. By entering a meditative or contemplative state and inviting the unconscious to provide insights, individuals may discover creative solutions to personal or professional challenges.

During the process, individuals can engage in inner dialogues with different aspects of themselves. For instance, someone might have an ongoing conversation between their conscious ego and their unconscious shadow, allowing for a deeper understanding of inner conflicts and unresolved issues.

The pendulum of the mind oscillates between sense and nonsense, not between right and wrong.

Jung's experiences during his 'psychotic break' prompted him to contemplate the nature of free will and the abstraction of thoughts. He recognized that our thoughts and beliefs are not purely products of rationality but are often influenced by deeper, unconscious forces. Jung's exploration of these themes contributed to his understanding of the complexity of human consciousness and the interplay between conscious and unconscious processes.

It was a pivotal moment in his life that propelled him into a deeper exploration of the unconscious and the mysteries of the human mind. It led to the development of his unique psychological theories, including concepts like active imagination and the collective unconscious, which continue to influence psychology and spirituality to this day.

His travels and encounters with various cultures also broadened his perspective and contributed to his holistic approach to understanding the human psyche. Prior to building the Bollingen Tower, Jung visited North Africa in 1920, where he spent time in Tunisia, Algeria and Egypt. During this trip, he had profound experiences and encounters that influenced his later work on psychology and symbolism.

VENTURING SOUTH OF EUROPE: JUNG IN NORTH AFRICA

And so Jung packed his luggage and headed down south. In 1920, Jung experienced a series of vivid dreams and visions while in North Africa. He documented these experiences in his diaries and later analysed them as essential components of his inner journey. His encounters with these symbolic dreams strengthened his belief in the importance of the unconscious mind in understanding human behaviour and personality.

Jung's exposure to North African mythology and folklore left a lasting impression on him. He studied the stories and myths of the local cultures, recognizing recurring motifs and archetypal themes that resonated with his broader theories. He commented that, 'The meeting of two personalities is like the contact of two chemical substances; if there is any reaction, both are transformed.'

He noted the prevalence of ancient symbols like the mandala, which he saw as representations of the human psyche's inner structure. Jung remarked that these symbols seemed to transcend cultural boundaries, leading him to formulate his theories on archetypes and the collective unconscious. He famously said, 'The dream is the small hidden door in the deepest and most intimate sanctum of the soul.'

During his visit to North Africa, Jung examined Europe through the eyes of what some considered a 'less developed' society. He was profoundly affected by the unhurried pace of life in North Africa, which stood in stark contrast to the relentless 'god of time' that seemed to dominate European (and, by implication, American) culture.

Jung hypothesized that this deliberate rhythm of life in North Africa allowed its people to lead more emotionally instinctive and intensely lived lives. He questioned whether the recent emergence of European rationality had come at the cost of diminished vitality. What did the rich, beautifully complex African culture capture that Europeans had yet to discover?

While in North Africa, Jung witnessed a peculiar work ritual involving multiple Bedouin tribes gathering to labour for a respected elder. Upon the elder's arrival, there was a cacophony of men shouting, dancing and playing small drums, seemingly entering unusual states of consciousness unfamiliar to Jung. The unified chanting resembled some sort of unified soul; a parallel to the collective unconscious.

As the work commenced, he observed men carrying heavy baskets of earth in a state of fervent excitement, dancing in harmony with the rhythmic beats of the drums. Jung admitted that, despite not intending to succumb to the allure of the primitive, he felt a psychic influence from the encounter. He even attributed a brief bout of infectious enteritis to this experience, which eventually resolved itself after a few days.

The wild shouts, dances and the hypnotic, trance-inducing effects of the pagan drums clearly stirred deep, unconscious sensations within Jung, causing him considerable distress and leading him to believe he had been physically affected by the potent psychic energies they stirred in people. There was power in the rhythms played with fervour and determination by the tribes and he amicably took part in these sessions during his journey.

Later in his African expedition, Jung had a revealing dream that shed some light on his anxious reaction to the tribal rites he had witnessed. In this dream, he found himself confronted by the image of an African American barber who had cut his hair during a trip to America 12 years prior.

In the dream, the barber held an intensely hot curling iron to Jung's head, intending to transform his hair into a kinky texture, resembling that of a person of African descent. Jung could vividly

Jung discusses an Egyptian artefact with Dr Carleton Smith, head of the National Arts Foundation of New York.

sense the searing heat and woke up filled with terror. He was undoubtedly ashamed of the lingering feelings of internalized racism.

He interpreted this dream as a warning from his unconscious mind, indicating that he perceived the primitive aspects within himself as a threat. At that moment, he believed he was perilously close to losing his own identity and succumbing to what he described as 'going black'. He wanted to move closer to his true self, rather than run away from it.

Jung noted that his unconscious mind had brought forth a memory of the barber, as a symbol to distract him from confronting the present and the disconcerting feelings it stirred within him. He wrote a long-winded, extraordinarily descriptive letter to his wife Emma during his trip:

After cold, heavy weather at sea, a sparkling morning in Algiers. Bright houses and streets, dark green clumps of trees, tall palms' crowns rising among them.

A patch of deep blue sky, a snow-white mosque dome; a shoemaker busily stitching away at shoes in a small vaulted niche, with a hot, dazzling, patch of sunlight on the mat before him.

Blind musicians with a hum and tiny three-stringed lute; a beggar who consists of nothing but rags; smoke from oil cakes, and swarms of flies; up above, on a white minaret in the blissful ether, a muezzin sings the midday chant...

Below, a cool, shady, colonnaded yard with horseshoe portal framed in glazed tiles; on the wall a mangy cat lies in the sun; coming and going of red, white, yellow, blue, brown mantles, white turbans, red fezzes, uniforms, faces ranging from white and light yellow to deep black...

On rolling, grey-green hills yellow-brown remains of whole Roman cities, small flocks of black goats grazing around them, nearby a Bedouin camp with blank tents, camels and donkeys.

Examining Jung's descriptions of African drumming rituals and his choice of language reveals his apprehension towards mob psychology. In his writings about the n'goma rituals in Sudan, Jung expresses concern, noting that in such dances accompanied by intense music, the natives easily succumb to a state of virtual possession.

This state of trance and possession represents the loss of individual will and the suspension of conscious awareness, both of which pose challenges within Jung's framework, especially in group dynamics. As the dancers intensify their ecstatic movements, Jung becomes increasingly alarmed, observing that 'as eleven o'clock approached, their excitement began to get out of bounds'.

In his perspective, the dancers gradually metamorphose into a frenzied horde, a transformation that deeply troubles him. The communal aspect of these ceremonies intrigued Jung, as they seemed to tap into a shared, primal aspect of the human psyche. However, despite his fascination, Jung also expressed apprehension about the potential for the loss of individuality within the collective experience.

Jung's fear of the crowd's seductive power prompts him to intervene decisively, putting an end to the affair with the crack of his whip. His encounter with the Bedouins further illustrates his concerns, as he observes a procession of 'hundreds of wild-looking men' moving in unison as if they were a single entity.

He believed that the unconscious forces at play in such group dynamics could lead to a kind of psychic contagion, where individuals might be swept up in the emotions and actions of the group, potentially leading to destructive or irrational behaviour. The early 20th century was marked by significant social and political upheavals, including the rise of totalitarian regimes, which further fuelled Jung's concerns about the potential negative consequences of unchecked collective forces.

Jung's choice of words, such as 'swarmed by', evokes the image of a mindless hive of worker bees, while describing the dancing men as a singular, fear-inducing 'horde' invokes negative historical associations with groups like Germanic tribes, invading Mongols, ravaging Huns and other violent collectives.

These descriptions clearly reflect Jung's opposition to the absorption of individuality by the masses and his characteristic Western emphasis on the value of individualism. He sees the value in a holistic, self-directed progression for each individual on their quest to become their most integrated, balanced self.

THE BOLLINGEN TOWER: A DREAM TURNED PALPABLE

Jung first purchased land in Bollingen in 1921, and initially built a small stone hut on the site. Over the years, he gradually added to the structure, incorporating additional rooms and features such as a kitchen, a library and a terrace. Jung built the now iconic landmark and tourist attraction Bollingen Tower using a variety of materials, including stones, wood and concrete.

Over the course of several years, Jung expanded and developed the original stone structure on the property, adding additional rooms, towers and a library. The Bollingen Tower became a symbol of Jung's individuation process – a physical manifestation of his inner journey and the integration of his unconscious and conscious selves.

> *Words and paper did not seem real enough to me. To put my fantasies on solid footing, something more was needed. I had to achieve a kind of representation in stone of my innermost thoughts and of the knowledge I had acquired.*

> *I wanted a room in this tower where I could exist for myself alone. I had in mind what I had seen in Indian houses, in which there is usually an area – though it may be only a corner of a room separated off by a curtain – in which the inhabitants can withdraw.*

The tower later became a significant symbol in Jungian psychology, representing the journey of individuation and the integration of the unconscious and conscious mind. He also incorporated many symbolic elements into the design, such as arches, spirals and the number four, which he believed represented wholeness and completeness. It served as a symbolic representation of his own individuation process, and he often used it as a space for contemplation and self-reflection.

The tower's intentional isolation and seclusion from urban life allowed Jung to immerse himself in contemplation. The tranquil environment, combined with the soothing sounds of the lake, created an atmosphere conducive to deep introspection. Bollingen became a physical embodiment of Jung's belief in the transformative power of solitude and communion with nature. The tower's distinctive turret offered panoramic vistas, further enhancing its appeal as a space for deep thought and inspiration.

Jung's direct involvement in the tower's construction is notable. He meticulously carved and inscribed many of the stones, infusing the structure with intricate symbols, mythological imagery, and references to his evolving psychological theories. The tower featured multiple levels, housing living quarters, a library, a study

Bollingen Tower, Jung's tangible construction of his psyche.

and spaces for artistic and creative pursuits. Its architectural design aimed to harmonize and emphasize a connection to nature.

Symbolic of transformation and the union of opposites, serpents and dragons were recurrent motifs in Jung's understanding of the psyche. These symbols can be found in various forms, such as sculptures, carvings and decorative elements in the tower. The cross and circle are archetypal symbols representing the union of opposites – the integration of spiritual and earthly realms. Jung included these in the tower's floor patterns.

The solar and lunar symbols were often associated with masculine and feminine energies, respectively, in Jungian psychology. The tower's architecture incorporated these symbols, including representations of the sun and moon in stained glass windows and other decorative elements. He emphasized the power of dualities and opposing forces, which is apparent in both smooth and sharp edges adorned and embellished within the interiors of the building.

Three out of four sides of a stone structure outside the tower are carved in either Greek or Latin. The first side, with the wall facing the tower, reads, *Here stands the mean, uncomely stone, Tis very cheap in price! The more it is despised by fools, the more loved by the wise.* This verse, authored by the Spanish alchemist Arnaldus de Villa Nova, alludes to the philosopher's stone, magnum opus, which stands as the ultimate aspiration for every alchemist – the lapis philosophorum.

The second carving on the wall features a mandala adorned with a depiction of Telesphorus of Asclepius (a figure from Greek mythology associated with healing and completion) positioned at its centre. Telesphorus, with his association with Asclepius, brings

Symbols carved into one of the four pillars gracing Bollingen Tower.

an element of therapeutic and transformative aspects to the overall symbolism of the carving.

Jung paid homage to this figure by inscribing a brief Greek message:

> [He] roams through the dark regions of this cosmos and glows like a star out of the depths. He points the way to the gates of the sun and to the land of dreams.

This passage emphasizes the importance of making amends with one's shadow and emerging out from the light at the end of the proverbial tunnel.

Jung's tower had its longest piece of carved writing facing the lake, possibly detailing his unconscious thoughts, which translates approximately to the following:

I am an orphan, alone; nevertheless I am found everywhere. I am one, but opposed to myself. I am youth and old man at one and the same time. Everyone's minds contain the symbols of the collective unconscious, which is referenced in the quote.

I have known neither father nor mother, because I have had to be fetched out of the deep like a fish, or fell like a white stone from heaven. In woods and mountains I roam, but I am hidden in the innermost soul of man. I am mortal for everyone, yet I am not touched by the cycle of aeons.

Jung made several modifications and additions to the Bollingen Tower over the years, reflecting his evolving interests, psychological insights, and the changing needs of the space. While the tower served as a retreat for Jung, it also became a canvas for his creative and symbolic expressions.

One notable modification was the expansion of the original tower, where Jung added additional rooms and spaces to accommodate his growing needs. These expansions not only enhanced the functionality of the space but also contributed to a more comfortable living and working environment.

A distinctive addition to the tower was a phallic symbol, representing the masculine principle. This addition reflects Jung's exploration of archetypal symbols and the integration of diverse elements into his personal and symbolic landscape.

Outside the tower, Jung placed a stone table and chair, creating an outdoor setting that provided him with a space for contemplation and reflection amid the natural surroundings. This choice highlighted Jung's appreciation for the connection between the human psyche and the natural world.

In remembrance of his lover, Toni Wolff, Jung installed a memorial stone with a Latin inscription that translated to 'She Conquered'. This addition added a poignant layer to the symbolism embedded within the tower, emphasizing the personal and emotional dimensions of Jung's relationship with the space.

Jung approached the construction and modification of the Bollingen Tower as an ongoing, creative process. For him, the tower was a living symbol of his psychological development, and the evolving nature of the tower mirrored Jung's commitment to personal growth and exploration – towards individuation.

Bollingen's legacy extends beyond its physical structure. Jung's extensive work on *The Red Book: Liber Novus*, a monumental exploration of his personal mythologies and psychological journey, took place within the confines of Bollingen. The tower and its surroundings significantly influenced Jung's psychological theories, particularly those related to the collective unconscious, archetypes and the individuation process.

After Jung's death in 1961, the Bollingen Foundation, established by Jung, took charge of the property. The tower and the surrounding property were eventually bequeathed to the Foundation. The Bollingen Foundation later became a part of the Philemon Foundation, which continues to manage the site.

As for public access, it's important to note that the Bollingen Tower is a private property, and public access is generally restricted.

However, there have been events and initiatives organized by the Philemon Foundation, such as conferences and seminars, that have allowed individuals interested in Jungian psychology to visit the site for specific purposes.

Today, Bollingen Tower remains a site of interest for scholars and enthusiasts of Jungian psychology, offering a glimpse into the intersection of architecture, symbolism and the inner workings of one of the most influential figures in the history of psychology. It serves as a unique tourist attraction for all people curious about the mystical workings of Jung's brain.

THE RED AND BLACK BOOKS

Jung spent approximately 16 years (1914–30) writing mental notes that streamed through his consciousness into the *Liber Novus* (Latin translation: New Book), which is known as *The Red Book* today. It had been unpublished until 2009, where Jung's extended family were convinced by scholar Dr Sonu Shamdasani to bring the mystical book to light. His musings were etched in black ink, coloured ink, as well as gouache paint.

The Red Book poses more questions than answers. In the 1920s, Jung expressed a looming sense of doubt as to whether his writing then could be understood or even unveiled to the public. After a whole decade of pondering, he reasoned that it had to be hidden – as no one would be able to interpret or even fathom what his mind was going through. It remains tucked away neatly in a bank vault in Zurich.

In alchemy the egg stands for the chaos apprehended by the artifex, the prima materia containing the captive world-soul.

A symbolic mandala from The Red Book.

Out of the egg – symbolized by the round cooking vessel – will rise the eagle or phoenix, the liberated soul, which is ultimately identical with the Anthropos who was imprisoned in the embrace of Physis.

During the same period, from November 1913 up to the early 1930s, Jung had seven journals which were called the 'Black Books', noted for exploring the darker parts of the psyche. Critics gave this period many names – from a psychotic break to a creative breakthrough. Whatever was happening to Jung, it certainly only happened to a select bunch of people in a century.

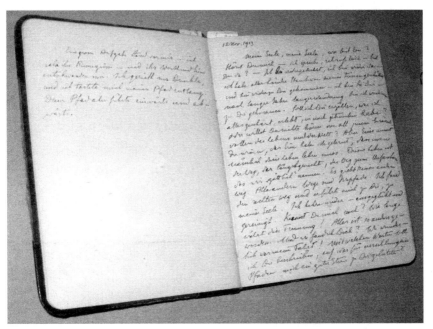

A page from one of Jung's Black Books.

The Black Books remained private during Jung's lifetime, but they were eventually published in 2020. The book includes facsimiles of Jung's original handwritten and illustrated pages, along with a transcription and translation. It provides a unique journey into Jung's personal exploration of the unconscious and the development of his psychological theories.

The first entry began with a cry out to his soul:

> *My soul, my soul, where are you? Do you hear me? I speak, I call you – are you there? I have returned, I am here again. I have shaken the dust of all the lands from my feet, and I have come to you, I am with you.*

FURTHER TRAVELS

In October of 1925, Jung and his friends took off to Eastern Kenya and Uganda with two of his colleagues, Franz Riklin and Ludwig Binswanger. He describes Mombasa as a picturesque and humidly hot settlement, tucked away in a forest of palm and mango trees. He developed a vested interest in the Polynesian and African concept of 'mana', which is a reference to a spiritual or supernatural power.

During their voyage, they encountered an Englishwoman named Ruth Bailey, who later joined them on a safari. Their expedition took them through the landscapes of Kenya and Uganda, eventually reaching the slopes of Mount Elgon. Jung's purpose for this expedition was to gain deeper insights into primitive psychology by engaging in conversations with inhabitants from culturally isolated regions in the area.

He was enchanted by his first sighting of a giant candelabrum cactus, which propelled him to continue exploring what other vegetation and livestock the peaceful village had to offer. He also witnessed the beauty of acacia trees, baobab trees, cacti, succulents, orchids, hibiscus and bougainvillea. These luscious and exotic plants caught his eye and influenced many of Jung's future dreams and visions.

There were herds of wild animals that ran across the desert: gazelle, antelope, gnu, zebra, warthog … and so many more. How remarkably different from Germany and America, Jung thought! The vegetation and ecosystems present were unlike anything he'd seen in the past. Wide-eyed in amazement, he proclaimed and detailed in his journal (which later became a part of his Black Books series):

Mount Elgon, a shield volcano in Uganda.

I walked away from my companions until I had put them out of sight, and savoured the feeling of being entirely alone. There I was now, the first human being to recognize that this was the world, but who did not know that in this moment he had first really created it.

There the cosmic meaning of consciousness became overwhelmingly clear to me. 'What nature leaves imperfect, the art perfects,' say the alchemists. Man, I, in an invisible act of creation put the stamp of perfection on the world by giving it objective existence.

This act we usually ascribe to the Creator alone, without considering that in so doing we view life as a machine calculated down to the last detail, which, along with the human psyche, runs on senselessly, obeying foreknown and predetermined rules.

Later the same year, in September, Jung visited Taos Pueblo in New Mexico, a small Native American community. He fully immersed himself in their culture and became more intrigued by spirituality, mythology and religion. He noted how the Indians would contemplate while wrapped in woollen blankets and serenely watch the wandering sun, without fail, each morning.

Jung actively participated in the rituals and ceremonies of the Taos Pueblo people. For instance, he attended their traditional dances, including the Buffalo Dance and the Deer Dance. These ceremonies were deeply spiritual and often connected to the cycles of nature, which fascinated Jung. Witnessing the precision and symbolism in these rituals left a lasting impression on him.

One example is the Buffalo Dance, where the dancers mimic the movements and behaviours of buffalo to invoke the spirit of these animals. Jung saw in this dance a profound connection between the Pueblo people's reverence for nature and his own theories about the collective unconscious and archetypal symbols. This experience reinforced his belief in the universality of certain symbols and myths across cultures.

Exactly a year earlier, he was invited to deliver a series of lectures at the University of New Mexico. During his trip, he learned the role of cultural context in shaping individual and collective psychology. Jung explored various rites of passages, rituals and practices that had shifted his worldview forever and

A Taos Pueblo village.

opened his eyes to an interconnectedness with Mother Earth.

> *In them there is a great deal that still belongs to the Middle Ages. Their Catholicism, for instance, is a strange mixture of Christian and pagan elements.*

> *Their religion is an original kind of pantheism, but there are also many other things in it. The gods appear to be partly personifications of natural forces, and partly personifications of psychic events.*

Jung connected with the Pueblo people (despite not knowing a single word in their mother tongue), and observed their rituals and ceremonies intently. He learned about 'kiva', which was a sacred chamber they used for religious ceremonies. In their dialect, it roughly translates to a large, circular underground room. Jung associated the space with a collective identity; a hidden purpose which was crucial for the human condition.

He attributed the dignity and calmness observed in the Pueblo Indians to their connection with the divine and their belief in the vital role of their rituals in maintaining the harmony of the universe. Jung interpreted the comments of Chief Mountain Lake about the restlessness of white individuals as indicative of their insatiable desire to exert dominance over every land and their megalomaniacal conviction that Christianity is the sole truth.

According to Jung, the religious and cosmological beliefs found in various cultures serve a valuable purpose by helping individuals imbue their existence with a sense of significance. Jung noted how the Pueblo Indians' beliefs were closely aligned with the

The Buffalo Dance, a Taos Pueblo custom.

naturalworld. Their reverence for the sun, the moon and other natural elements was not just a matter of religious practice but a way of connecting with the rhythms of nature.

A MEETING WITH CHIEF MOUNTAIN LAKE

He also had a professional relationship with Taos Pueblo leader Ochwiay Biano (known as Chief Mountain Lake) as they delved deep into the experience of the *other* (non-whites), which today, would be considered a culturally controversial conversation. Jung recalled having been able to converse with the chief unlike any European he'd ever spoken with. Jung wanted to dive head-first into the multi-layered, gorgeously complex culture of the Pueblo people.

Chief Mountain Lake: 'See how cruel the whites look, their lips are thin, their noses sharp, their faces furrowed and distorted by folds. Their eyes have a staring expression; they are always seeking something. What are they seeking? The whites always want something. They are always uneasy and restless. We do not know what they want. We do not understand them. We think that they are all mad.'

When Jung asked why he thinks they are all mad, Mountain Lake replied, 'They say they think with their heads.'

'Why of course,' said Jung, 'what do you think with?'

'We think here,' said Chief Mountain Lake, indicating his heart.

The primary lesson Jung took away from his encounter with Mountain Lake emphasized the significance of constructing meaning through a coherent belief system and corresponding practices. Jung regarded the specific content of these belief systems as of secondary importance. He underscored that while diverse cultures may hold distinct belief systems, there's no definitive way to ascertain which, if any, is the absolute truth.

Jung seemed to assert that the specific belief system itself holds less importance than the common outcome it yields – a profound sense of meaning and purpose in the lives of those who embrace it. In a way, Jung was a psychological consequentialist and considered the end result from personal reflections such as shadow work (learning how to manage one's hidden impulses) to be more important than one's initial motivations for doing so.

Every culture or subculture possesses its unique set of beliefs and practices that offer a sense of purpose and understanding. These belief systems need not necessarily be religious; even an agnostic or atheist perspective can provide an individual with a personally meaningful outlook on existence.

Jung was intrigued by the idea of developing a theory that integrated Pueblo psychology into his existing theory of personality types. His visit with Mountain Lake stimulated his reflections on how various cultures place differing values on thinking and feeling, akin to the diversity of individuals within a culture.

Inspired by Mountain Lake's assertion that Indians relied on their hearts for thinking rather than their heads, Jung hypothesized a profound contrast between white and Indian psychologies, expressing an apparent admiration for the psychological orientation of Indian culture.

Jung's encounter with the Native Americans in New Mexico remained a deeply ingrained memory. Following their initial encounter, Jung and Mountain Lake engaged in a correspondence. In a letter penned to Mountain Lake several years after his visit, Jung conveyed his ongoing exploration of the truths held dear by the Native American community, emphasizing his profound admiration for these beliefs. (Berger & Segaller, 2000, p. 137.)

Mountain Lake expressed in one of his letters the idea that the paramount duty of the Pueblo people was to assist the sun, their revered Father, who sustains the entire world. He reiterated the importance of each person's body–nature connection.

Jung was profoundly affected by this sentiment and noted in his own writings that his Native American friend from the Pueblo believed that the Pueblo's purpose was to aid the sun's journey across the sky, and he felt a sense of longing for the profound depth of meaning inherent in such a belief.

Could humanity, as a whole, be more alike than different? Does everyone share core desires, deep down? Jung believed the symbols he encountered were universal and reflected deep-seated aspects of the human psyche that stood the test of time. These symbols were also consistent among different cultures and groups of people.

SYMBOLISM IN THE PUEBLO CULTURE

Kivas, for example, represented the womb of Mother Earth and the connection between spiritual and physical realms. They are large, circular rooms that are situated underground for ceremonial purposes. The elaborate rituals and symbols created by the Pueblo people were, essentially, manifestations of their collective unconscious.

Kivas were ingeniously designed structures. Typically, they had a small, round hole in the floor or wall, known as the sipapu, which symbolized the portal through which their ancestors entered this world. This architectural feature emphasized the connection between the kiva and the spirit world. Ladders or hatches provided access to the kiva from the surface, and their orientation often followed celestial alignments, further tying them to the cosmos.

The circular shape of kivas symbolized the cyclical nature of life, death and rebirth. It mirrored the Pueblo people's agricultural and seasonal cycles, reinforcing their deep connection to the Earth and the natural world. Additionally, the circle represented unity and equality among community members, emphasizing the importance of collective harmony in their way of life.

Kivas served as sacred spaces where intricate rituals and ceremonies were conducted. These ceremonies were essential for maintaining harmony in the physical and spiritual realms, ensuring successful crops, and fostering communal cohesion. Ceremonial objects and paraphernalia were stored within the kiva, adding to its significance as a spiritual hub.

Their architecture, typically subterranean or partly underground, symbolized the connection between the human realm and the sacred depths of the Earth. This design was not only practical for temperature regulation but also held profound spiritual meaning, emphasizing the importance of maintaining harmony with the natural world. The sacred act of descending into a kiva was seen as a symbolic journey into the Earth's womb, a place

A kiva, symbolizing the womb of Mother Earth.

where individuals could connect with the profound forces of creation and renewal.

Moreover, kivas were the sites for transmitting cultural knowledge and traditions from one generation to the next. Elders and spiritual leaders would pass down their wisdom, stories and sacred rituals within the confines of these hallowed spaces. This intergenerational exchange ensured the preservation of cultural heritage and maintained a strong sense of identity within the community.

One of the most important symbols that Jung encountered among the Pueblo people was the kachina, which are spirit beings that play a central role in Pueblo religious ceremonies. Jung saw the kachina as an embodiment of the archetype of the wise old man, a figure that appears in many cultures and represents wisdom, guidance and the search for meaning.

Among the Pueblo people, the kachina spirits are seen as intermediaries between the human world and the spiritual realm. They are believed to possess profound knowledge and the ability to guide and protect the community. Kachinas are often depicted as masked figures, and their rituals involve elaborate dances and ceremonies. These ceremonies serve as a means of connecting with the kachina spirits to seek their wisdom and blessings.

Jung's exploration of the kachina and its connection to the wise old man archetype underscores his belief in the interconnectedness of human psychology and cultural expression. He argued that these archetypal symbols arise from the deep well of the collective unconscious, reflecting fundamental aspects of the human experience that transcend individual cultures and time periods.

Another important symbol that Jung encountered among the Pueblo people was the Sun Dance, which is a complex ritual that involves dancing, fasting and self-mortification. Jung saw the Sun Dance as a symbol of the journey of individuation, in which an individual goes through a process of self-discovery and transformation.

The Sun Dance is a demanding and transformative ritual that often lasts for several days. Participants undergo physical and emotional challenges, including fasting and piercing their flesh with wooden skewers. These are not merely acts of self-infliction but are deeply symbolic, representing the willingness to endure hardship and suffering in pursuit of a higher purpose.

The sacred ceremony is closely tied to the symbolism of the sun, a universal symbol of illumination, enlightenment and renewal. The sun's daily journey across the sky mirrors the individual's quest for self-discovery and transformation. Just as the sun rises each day, the participants in the Sun Dance aspire to rise to new levels of consciousness and self-realization.

Jung also found significance in the Pueblo's use of sand paintings, which are intricate designs made of coloured sand that are used in healing rituals. Jung saw the sand paintings as a reflection of the mandala, a symbol of wholeness and integration that is found in many cultures and is often used in Jungian therapy.

The Pueblo Indians, who primarily reside in the south-western United States, create intricate sand paintings as part of their religious and healing rituals. These paintings are made by carefully pouring coloured sand on to a flat surface to create complex, symmetrical designs. The purpose of these sand paintings is to invoke the aid of spiritual forces, to heal the sick, and to restore balance and harmony within the community.

A kachina doll, representative of a Hopi deity or spirit.

THE SECRET OF THE GOLDEN FLOWER – A CHINESE PERSPECTIVE

In 1928, Jung read *The Secret of the Golden Flower* – an esoteric guide to Chinese meditation methods – as translated by his friend, Richard Wilhelm. It dates back to the late Tang Dynasty (AD 618–907). The year after, in 1929, he wrote a foreword for the book, where he boldly states, 'Eternal is the Golden Flower only, which grows out of inner liberation from all bondage to things. A man who reaches this stage transposes his ego; he is no longer limited to the monad [a singular unit or entity], but penetrates the magic circle of the polar duality of all phenomena and returns to the undivided *One, Tao*.' He also touched upon the importance of *hsing* (essence/logos), and *ming* (life) in understanding the text.

Jung came across this ancient text through his studies of Eastern wisdom and saw it as a valuable source of insights into the human psyche. He believed that the symbols and teachings found in *The Secret of the Golden Flower* resonated with concepts he had encountered in his own psychoanalytic work.

In his analysis of *The Secret of the Golden Flower*, Jung observed that the Chinese alchemical symbols of the 'diamond body' and the 'holy fruit' represent the purified, incorruptible breath-body or spirit-body that Taoist practitioners seek in their pursuit of spiritual immortality. Jung believed that these concepts had broader significance for humanity, especially in the later stages of life.

I have reason to believe that this attitude sets in after Middle Life and is a natural preparation for death. Chinese

A painting of the golden flower mandala by one of Jung's patients.

yoga philosophy is based on this instinctive preparation
for death as a goal.

Under the laws of Taoism, Jung equated *hun (yang/light)* to his animus and *p'o (yin/shadow)* to his anima. He said the animus dwells in the eyes of a person, whereas the anima is nestled in the abdomen. The animus is 'bright and active'; the anima 'dark and earth-bound'. Self-actualization can loosely be translated to a person's ability to *shen,* or rise spiritually.

Jung's interest in the book intensified during his period of personal crisis, which he later referred to as his 'confrontation with the unconscious'. This crisis led to the formulation of his theories on individuation, the process of integrating the conscious and unconscious aspects of the self to achieve wholeness and self-realization.

Jung saw parallels with his concept of the self, which represents the totality of the psyche, encompassing both the conscious and unconscious aspects of an individual. The 'Golden Flower' symbolizes the highest state of spiritual realization. Jung saw this as analogous to the philosopher's stone in alchemy, which represents the fully developed and integrated Self.

Moreover, Jung explored the alchemical symbolism present in *The Secret of the Golden Flower*. Alchemy, both in the Western and Eastern traditions, is seen as a spiritual process of transformation, wherein base elements are transmuted into higher forms, reflecting the journey of the soul towards enlightenment or self-realization.

The circular movement described in *The Secret of the Golden Flower* can be seen as a representation of the ongoing process of self-exploration and understanding, similar to Jung's idea of circumambulation in alchemy. Both texts depict a continuous journey of self-discovery and growth, where an individual delves into the depths of their psyche to find wholeness and inner harmony.

Jung saw the alchemical process as a metaphor for the journey of self-discovery, inner growth and integration of the unconscious. By drawing connections between Eastern wisdom and Western psychology, Jung expanded the understanding of human consciousness and provided a bridge between different cultural and philosophical traditions, enriching the depth and applicability of his psychological theories.

The Secret of the Golden Flower also includes instructions for meditative practices, and Jung recognized the value of such techniques in achieving a transcendent state of consciousness. Meditation, for Jung, was a means of accessing the deeper layers of the unconscious and fostering inner transformation.

In the exploration of Jung's interpretation of *The Secret of the Golden Flower*, it becomes evident that Jung found in this Taoist text a rich source of inspiration and resonance with his own psychological theories. The symbolism of the Golden Flower as a representation of the self, the integration of opposites, and the emphasis on a circular movement akin to the mandala, all align with Jung's concepts of individuation and the quest for wholeness.

Jung's engagement with this Eastern wisdom not only illustrates his openness to diverse cultural perspectives but also underscores his belief in the universality of certain archetypal themes that transcend geographical and cultural boundaries.

STRIFE AND SEPARATION FROM EMMA

Throughout the 1920s, Jung's marriage to Emma had been troubled with jealousy, distance and differing values. They separated in the late 1920s, and were formally divorced in 1934 owing partly to Jung's increasing involvement in his work and his growing interest in philosophical ideas that diverged from those of his colleagues and peers. Emma was deeply sceptical of Jung's ideas and felt increasingly marginalized and unsupported in their marriage.

In one letter to Emma, dated 13 January 1933, Jung wrote: 'We have had to part from each other, and that is bitter. But I think we can console ourselves with the thought that we did what we could and had to do. We are both human and have our limitations, and we cannot always succeed in doing what we wish.' He still wished her the best and harboured no ill feelings towards their time together.

In another (more optimistic) letter, dated 15 February 1933, Jung expressed his hope that their separation would allow both of them to find greater personal and professional fulfilment. He wrote: 'I am certain that both of us will find new paths, new experiences, and new insights in the future. We have both grown in our own ways, and we must continue to do so.' Jung thought this tough decision would help them both become self-actualized versions of themselves.

Jung's relationship with his colleague Toni Wolff also contributed to the strain on his marriage. Although he remained married to Emma, Jung had a deep emotional and intellectual connection with Wolff that at times bordered on romantic entanglement. This caused significant tension and conflict within all three of their personal lives.

After the separation, Jung continued to maintain contact with Emma, and the two remained professional, cordial and respectful towards each other. However, they never reconciled. Their official split allowed him to explore new ideas and interests more freely, and it was a crucial turning point in his personal and professional development.

Looking back, on Valentine's Day in 1903, Carl Jung and Emma Rauschenbach tied the knot. Over the initial 11 years of their marriage, they welcomed five children into their family. Shortly after their wedding, Agathe, their first child, arrived, followed by Anna Margaretha (known as Gret) just 14 months later. Their only son, Franz, was born in November 1908, and they later had two more daughters, Marianne (born in September 1910) and Helene (born in March 1914).

Jung, in one of his numerous letters to Freud, mentioned their efforts to prevent further pregnancies, which didn't seem to be very successful. Following 1914, it became customary for the Jungs to have separate bedrooms, as was typical for individuals of their social standing with fully grown families.

Carl Jung in 1935.

However, the end of his marriage also came with significant emotional pain and turmoil – which he detailed in his private journals:

I am a divided personality, and my wife suffers most from my other side. I live in a world of ideas and visions, while she lives in a world of material reality. We are like two ships passing in the night, and the distance between us seems to grow wider every day.

Emma held a profound emotional attachment to Jung and longed to establish a deep connection built on both physical desire and shared intellectual pursuits. However, Jung was evasive in this regard. Emma had a keen understanding of the situation and expressed to Freud that her husband used the excuse of needing to earn a living, while it was apparent that there was an underlying issue to which he was resistant.

This 'something' may have been connected to Jung's mother complex, causing him to be cautious about becoming too emotionally entwined and allowing 'The Mother' to exert too much influence over him. Jung's avoidance had a significant consequence: he excluded Emma from his inner world. She was denied access to his Black Books and was never privy to his introspective endeavours.

Consequently, she was never his trusted confidante, which inflicted deep emotional wounds and humiliation upon her. As Jung's professional and social life became more intricate and his fame extended throughout Europe and America, Emma was increasingly marginalized. She found herself relegated to the periphery while other admirers and associates, whom she referred to as 'Valkyries', held Jung in high regard. In her eyes, she was merely confined to the role of the wife, distanced from the inner circle.

'Kinder, Küche, Kirche', which translates to 'children, kitchen, church', encapsulates the traditional German housewife roles. Emma managed to fulfil the first two, concerning children and the kitchen, but neither she nor Jung held much interest in organized religion, and their children were not confirmed as a result. In this aspect, they were more 'progressive' than the majority of Swiss parents of their time.

Despite facing various challenges, including hurtful behaviours, slights, infidelity and indignities that modern women might find difficult to tolerate, Emma remained composed and dignified throughout. She observed from the sidelines, displaying the demeanour of a queen – calm, collected and reserved, often described as 'serene' – even as Jung attracted the attention of admirers.

While the end of their marriage was a sombre event, it paved the way for new opportunities, personal growth and continued contributions to the world of psychology for both Carl and Emma Jung. Their legacy as pioneers in the field of psychology endures, and their work continues to inspire and influence generations of researchers, therapists and thinkers.

Middle Life, as a whole, serves as the crucible for the emergence of wisdom and a deeper understanding of one's true self. Jung's concept of individuation takes centre stage as people grapple with the integration of unconscious elements, and strive for a more authentic and fulfilling life. Characterized by the exploration of existential questions and the pursuit of meaning, it sets the groundwork for a continued quest for psychic wholeness.

CHAPTER 5

OLD AGE

Jung's stage of Old Age unfolds as a poignant exploration of the twilight years in his comprehensive psychological framework. The phase represents a culmination of a lifelong journey towards individuation, where the accumulated experiences, reflections and integrations of the self reveal themselves at the forefront.

Individuals at this stage face the prospect of the ultimate integration: the acceptance of life and its end in its entirety. In the last chapter of life, people must face the challenge of finding meaning, transcending their ego's limitations, and cultivating a profound sense of wisdom that reaches beyond the temporal aspects of existence.

TRAVELS TO INDIA AND CEYLON

December 1937 marked the start of Jung's three-month trip to India and Ceylon (modern-day Sri Lanka) with over a hundred scientists to celebrate the Silver Jubilee of the Association of the Indian Science Congress hosted by the British Association for the Advancement of Science in Calcutta (modern-day Kolkata).

It's essential to keep in mind that Jung's visit to India took place during the winter of 1937–38, subsequent to the publication of the *Prabuddha Bharata* article, which detailed the many facets of Indian spirituality. It's possible that Jung's concepts underwent changes due to his visit to India, particularly his experience at Belur Math.

Jung was notably impressed by the statue of Sri Ramakrishna at Belur Math. He later observed that the term 'samadhi' would likely evoke the image of a yogi in that state for any Indian. As time passed, Jung's thinking evolved, and he started to view the East and West not as opposing forces but rather as parallel paths. This shift in his thoughts marked a maturation of his ideas.

He started his journey in Bombay, where he was greeted at the Taj Mahal hotel. He then travelled through Hyderabad, Aurangabad, Daulatabad, Sanchi, Delhi Fort, Qutub Minar, Masjid, the Shah Jahan palace, Diwan I Khas, then Dehra Dun.

From there, he travelled to the ancient city of Benares, where he studied Hindu philosophy and spirituality and met with local scholars and spiritual leaders. He remarked that throughout this journey through India, he truly explored the most important experiences of his life that undoubtedly shaped his worldview and opinions.

On 27 December, Jung arrived at the Banaras Hindu University in Benares, where he dejectedly said, 'I cannot stand this any longer, I want to return to the hotel.' He could no longer stand the sullen 'grimness' of the city. Jung craved new, mind-opening experiences; Benares was 'flat' and 'lifeless' in his eyes.

After almost a month, his crew headed towards Calcutta, where he gave several lectures on his theories of analytical psychology at the University of Calcutta in January 1938. Afterwards, he went to Madras, then Mysore, Trichur, Trivandrum, and Colombo.

Afterwards, Jung and his group travelled to Ceylon, where they visited several important Buddhist sites, including the ancient city of Anuradhapura and the Temple of the Tooth in Kandy. Jung was particularly interested in the concept of the 'Buddha-nature', which he saw as a parallel to his own idea of the self as a central organizing principle of the psyche.

The Indian's goal is not moral perfection, but the condition of nirdvandva; he wishes to free himself from nature; in keeping with this aim, he seeks in meditation the condition of imagelessness and emptiness.

The stupas are tombs or containers of relics, hemispherical in shape, like two gigantic rice bowls placed one on top of the other (concavity upon concavity), according to the prescripts of the Buddha himself in the Mahaparinibbana-Sutta.

The drum speaks the ancient language of the belly and solar plexus; the belly does not 'pray' but engenders the meritorious mantram or meditative utterance.

After their visit to Ceylon and the Colombo Port, Jung and his group returned to India and travelled to several other cities, including Delhi, Bombay (now Mumbai) and Pune. Jung was especially interested in the work of the Indian spiritual leader Sri Aurobindo, whom he visited in his ashram in Pondicherry.

Jung and Aurobindo had several discussions on the nature of consciousness and the potential for human transformation, which had a significant impact on Jung's later work. Aurobindo was known for his diplomatic views on human nature, and said, 'To hate the sinner is the worst sin, for it is hating God; yet he who

The famous statue of Ramakrishna at Belur Math.

commits it glories in his superior virtue.'

Aurobindo also described the then burgeoning field of psychology as 'an infant science ... which has the universal habit of the human mind to take partial or local truths, generalize them unduly and try to explain the whole field of human nature in its narrow terms.' He opened Jung's eyes to the different soul types, and observed that Western psychology and yoga were gradually enmeshing together.

Jung's journey to the Silver Jubilee Indian Science Congress did not go as anticipated. Despite his expectations, he discovered no connections with fellow psychologists in India or the broader scientific community, raising suspicions that the invitation for his visit might have originated from British authorities rather than the Indian intellectual elite.

Unfortunately, Jung had been misled into believing that his ideas were familiar to a certain group, but it became evident during the event that they were entirely unknown in India. To his dismay, the congress showcased a deliberate and prominent alignment with Freudian theories, further distancing Jung from the prevailing intellectual atmosphere.

From the very start of his journey, Freud's followers displayed opposition towards Jung, catching him off guard and leaving the northern part of his visit to India dissatisfied on a personal level. However, the second part of Jung's expedition to southern India was a deeply personal and transformative experience.

Exploring southern India provided Jung with an opportunity to juxtapose the beliefs he had developed through years of study with the region's art and architecture, uncovering profound messages within them, for the betterment of humanity as a whole.

A temple in Anuradhapura – the anciety city holds several important Buddhist sites.

FURTHER COLLABORATIONS WITH FAMOUS SCIENTISTS

Starting in 1941, Károly Kerényi, a Hungarian scholar known for his work in comparative mythology, began delivering lectures at the Eranos conferences in Ascona, Switzerland. These conferences came about due to an invitation from Carl Gustav Jung and provided a platform for both scholars to share their insights and engage with a wider audience interested in psychology, mythology and spirituality.

The ongoing interaction with the Swiss psychologist initiated Kerényi's link with Switzerland, ultimately resulting in his decision to permanently settle in the Italian-speaking canton of Ticino. Kerényi also taught courses on Hungarian language and literature at the University of Basel.

In 1949, Jung collaborated with Kerényi for *Essays on a Science of Mythology: the Myth of the Divine Child and the Mysteries of Eleusis*. In this book, Jung focused upon the psychology of the child archetype, where he draws connections between Greek, Roman, Indian, Finnish and other cultures.

The underpinning of synchronicity becomes more apparent when we consider Kerényi's active involvement, effectively expanding the original Jung–Kerényi duo into a trio, with the addition of Wolfgang Pauli, an Austrian theoretical physicist. Central to this discussion is the dynamic interplay between the conscious and unconscious mind.

A prominent element of this unique communication revolves around the patterns found in the Eleusinian Mysteries, the archetypal representation of the Mother and Daughter, and the in-depth examination of this as a dynamic hermeneutical system.

Kerényi, as a scholar of mythology, delved into various mythologies, with a particular focus on Greece. He examined the archetypal representation of the Mother and Divine Child in Greek myths and rituals. This archetype is exemplified in the story of Demeter (the Mother) and Persephone (the Divine Child), where Persephone is abducted to the underworld and then reunited with her mother, symbolizing the cycle of life, death and rebirth.

Jung expanded on Kerényi's mythological insights and incorporated them into his theory of archetypes. Jung's concept of archetypes involves universal, innate symbols and themes found in the collective unconscious of humanity. The Mother and Divine Child archetype, as seen in various mythologies, was a central component of this theory.

Jungian psychology emphasizes that the Mother and Divine Child archetype represents a profound psychological pattern within the human psyche. The Mother symbolizes the nurturing, protective and life-giving aspects of the unconscious, while the Divine Child represents the potential for growth, renewal and transformation. This archetype is one of the main symbols of the individuation process – the 'mascot' of self-realization.

By recognizing the cognitive connections between the conscious and unconscious minds within this triad of individuals (Jung, Pauli, and Kerényi), we uncover an unconscious and acausal synchronistic phenomenon as well.

Jung noted that the primitive mentality 'does not think consciously', rather, that 'thoughts appear'. Children must put themselves in the 'mood of willing' in order to exert psychic effort, as they are unable to do so consciously. They are still unable to self-reflect, and this translates to them giving in to impulses without a second thought.

> *[A man] may have violently separated himself from his original character in the interests of some arbitrary persona more in keeping with his ambitions. He has thus become unchildlike and artificial, and lost his roots.*

Jung highlighted the paradoxical motif that 'smaller than small, yet bigger than big' represents how impotence is shown through children and ultimately the hero's journey. The hero themself can power through multiple obstacles, yet be completely powerless after encountering the slightest undoing.

He suggests that a 'child' is destined (and unconsciously pulled) towards independence, and to do so, they must detach themself

A statue depicting the abduction of the Greek goddess Persephone.

from their origins. A bird must leave its nest; an adult must learn how to sustain their life without their parents. Jung also warns that progress and development 'lose all meaning' if someone only grows into a new state as a 'fragment' of themself.

Jung suggests that the child archetype attempts to separate themself from their identity with the role of the 'hero', which is a grandiose delusion to guard their ego. He likens the experience of the child to a 'conviction that one is extraordinary, or else the impossibility of pretension only proves one's inferiority, which is favourable to the role of the heroic sufferer'.

Ironically enough, Jung observes that someone cannot have an inflated sense of self without simultaneously feeling inferior due to self-esteem issues. In other words, arrogance is not a stand-alone trait – it must be coupled with a deep-seated sense of inferiority due to the wounded ego.

In addition, the Eleusinian Mysteries were a set of secretive religious rites and rituals that took place in ancient Greece, centred around the worship of Demeter and Persephone. These mysteries were known for their secrecy and their promise of spiritual enlightenment and a favourable afterlife.

The myth of Persephone's abduction by Hades and her subsequent return to the surface world is a central theme. It's seen as an allegory for the human soul's journey into the depths of the unconscious (the underworld) and its eventual return to conscious awareness. This journey mirrors the cycle of death and rebirth.

Moreover, Jung and Kerényi's psychological interpretation of these myths reveals their relevance for individuation – the process of becoming whole and integrating the various facets of the self. The Eleusinian Mysteries, with their promise of spiritual enlightenment and understanding, are seen as a profound initiation into the mysteries of existence.

This in depth essay invites readers to recognize that ancient myths are not merely relics of the past but serve as a rich source of wisdom and insight into the human condition. It illustrates how mythology, as a reflection of the collective unconscious, continues to inform and enrich our understanding of the complexities of human consciousness.

In essence, *The Myth of the Divine Child and the Mysteries of Eleusis* reminds us that the pursuit of self-awareness and the quest for meaning are age-old endeavours deeply rooted in our shared mythic heritage. It encourages us to explore the depths of our own psyches, just as the initiates of Eleusis ventured into the underworld, in the hope of discovering profound truths about ourselves and the world we inhabit.

SEEKING THE WAYS AND SPIRITUAL KNOWLEDGE OF THE DIVINE

Jung also immersed himself in the rich culture and religions of Buddhism and Islam. He observed that India offered a markedly different way of civilizing their citizens with peace, as opposed to violence or secularism. This stark contrast compelled him to conduct some further investigation through their sacred texts.

In his study of Buddhism, he found inspiration in its emphasis on inner peace, mindfulness and the pursuit of enlightenment as a path to individual and societal harmony. His exploration of Islam exposed him to the principles of submission to a higher power, compassion and the interconnectedness of all living beings.

These experiences broadened his understanding of diverse approaches to spiritual fulfilment and provided valuable insights into the potential for well-balanced, peaceful societies.

Buddhism has the characteristics of a mass movement. It rose at a time when religious and philosophical speculations had made a general impression on the minds of men, and when the old religions no longer sufficed.

The spirit of Islam is intellectually liberal, tolerant and friendly to science.

[Islam] is a religion with an enormous power of expansion, and as I see it, Islam is essentially a political system which is partly religious and only in part does it rest on ethical principles.

Although Jung was opposed to the dogmatism of religion, he was a highly spiritual fellow who appreciated the interconnectedness of the human condition. He was meticulous in his observations about various doctrines and faiths he'd encountered. Through his journey, Jung kept a detailed journal of his experiences, which he later published as *Psychology and the East*.

In *Psychology and the East*, Jung documented his encounters with various Eastern philosophies and spiritual practices, such as Zen Buddhism, Hinduism and Taoism. He was particularly drawn to the concept of individuation and self-realization, which he found resonated with ideas present in many Eastern traditions.

Jung's exploration of the East expanded his understanding of the human psyche and the potential for spiritual growth and self-transformation. His work in this area not only enriched his own inner journey but also contributed to the broader dialogue between Western psychology and Eastern spirituality.

Jung's willingness to bridge the gap between psychology and spirituality remains a significant aspect of his legacy. His work emphasized the importance of recognizing the interconnectedness of the human condition and the role of spirituality in the process of self-discovery. To do so, one must recognize their internal imbalances and contradictions and work towards balance.

In doing so, he provided a valuable perspective for individuals seeking to navigate the complexities of their inner worlds while acknowledging the diverse tapestry of spiritual beliefs and practices that shape our understanding of human consciousness. The soul and psyche is an ever-evolving ecosystem that ultimately affects the course of each person's life.

Jung's work resonates with those who understand that human existence is not solely defined by empirical data or objective observations. Instead, he encouraged a holistic view that encompasses the spiritual and transcendent dimensions of our lives. By doing so, he contributed to a broader understanding of human nature, one that goes beyond reductionist, materialistic perspectives.

Moreover, Jung's work recognizes and respects the rich diversity of spiritual beliefs and practices that shape our understanding of human consciousness. He steered clear of advocating for a specific religious doctrine or dogma and instead encouraged individuals to engage with their own spirituality in a way that resonated with their unique experiences.

He makes a bold remark, 'It is quite possible that India is the real world and that the white man lives in a madhouse of abstractions.'

The stone was a 'little world' like man himself, a sort of inner image of the cosmos, reaching not into immeasurable distances but into an equally immeasurable depth-dimension (i.e., from the small to the unimaginably smallest).

Jung recognized the limitations of rational knowledge when it comes to understanding the transcendent or the divine. He acknowledged the existence of a spiritual realm beyond ordinary consciousness, which he referred to as 'the numinous'. Essentially, every individual could have their own direct experiences of the numinous through religious or mystical encounters.

Throughout his life, he explored a variety of different religions, faiths and sects to gain a better understanding of the spiritual plane. The most influential ones were Christianity, Taoism, Buddhism, Hinduism, Islam, Judaism and indigenous faiths from all around the world – the Americas, Africa, Australia, Polynesia and even the Arctic regions.

By studying diverse religious systems, Jung sought to uncover the underlying universality of human consciousness. His rigorous enquiry into these religions allowed him to weave a comprehensive tapestry of human spirituality, enriching his analytical psychology and offering invaluable insights into the intricate tapestry of human existence, meaning and self-discovery.

Through this extraordinary journey, Jung illuminated the perennial quest for meaning and individuation that lies at the core of the human soul, inspiring generations to explore the depths of their own inner worlds and connect with the diverse spiritual fabric that unites humanity across time and space.

JUNG'S DETERIORATING VITALITY AND HIS REFLECTIONS

In 1944, Jung suffered from a heart attack, which was so serious that he was near death, and for a while, it was uncertain whether he would survive. During his recovery, Jung was forced to take a break from his work as a practising psychologist, which gave him time to reflect on his life and work and to write about his experiences. He eventually resigned from his tenure as a professor of medical psychology at the University of Basel.

One of the key insights that Jung gained from his experience of illness was the importance of attending to the body as well as the mind in the process of healing. He realized that physical symptoms and illnesses could be manifestations of unconscious psychological processes, and that by attending to the body, it was possible to gain insight into the underlying psychological issues.

Jung also came to see his heart attack as a kind of psychological initiation or transformation, a process that he had explored in his earlier work on alchemy and the process of individuation. He ultimately saw his illness as a kind of alchemical process, in which he was forced to confront and integrate aspects of his unconscious psyche in order to heal and transform. His gripping health conditions continued...

He later fell physically ill in 1952 with various cardiovascular diseases, including angina (chest pain) and arrhythmia (irregular heartbeat). These conditions were related to his earlier heart attack in 1944 and were likely exacerbated by his age and the chronic stress of his work as one of the country's most famous and renowned psychiatrists. He also sported a few battle scars while he ploughed through the grey area of patient–therapist relationships.

During his health struggles, Jung's mind was still haunted by images of sins he'd committed in the past, such as transference with multiple patients even though he was married to a devoted wife. Jung desperately tried to jump in head-first, dive into the deepest crevices of his thoughts, and understand what was going on. There may have been a sense of a mind–body duality going on for Jung. Poor mental health, it seemed, also directly had an impact on his physical health.

In 1945, Jung wrote extensively on the shadow, which is 'the thing a person has no wish to be'. Each person can choose to confront their personal shadow and emerge on the other end of understanding with inner peace, or choose to ignore it. The shadow self, nestled in the unconscious, is often ridden with intense feelings of guilt and shame. Personal triggers or traumas may cause these thoughts to rise to the surface momentarily.

In myths, the hero is the one who conquers the dragon, not the one who is devoured by it. And yet both have to deal with the same dragon. Also, he is no hero who never met the dragon, or who, if once he saw it, declared afterwards that he saw nothing.

Equally, only one who has risked the fight with the dragon and is not overcome by it wins the hoard, the 'treasure to attain'. He alone has a genuine claim to self-confidence, for he has faced the dark ground of his self and thereby has gained himself.

Despite his ongoing health problems, Jung continued to be a prolific writer, researcher and thinker. He produced several important works during this period, including *Answer to Job* (1952) and *Synchronicity: An Acausal Connecting Principle* (1952). In these works, he explored new ideas about the nature of the psyche and the relationship between the individual and the collective unconscious.

Everything now depends on man: immense power of destruction is given into his hand, and the question is whether he can resist the will to use it, and can temper his will with the spirit of love and wisdom. He will hardly be capable of doing so on his own unaided resources.

WHEN PHYSICS GREETS PSYCHOLOGY

Jung started writing the book *The Interpretation of Nature and the Psyche* with physicist Wolfgang Pauli in 1950. It was originally published in German in 1952 as *Naturerklärung und Psyche: Die unbewussten Kräfte in der Wissenschaft* and later translated into English. It elegantly ties together the patterns between science and psychology – the archetypes and collective unconscious with matter and energy.

Pauli focused on how Jung's archetypal ideas tie in with the scientific theories of German astronomer Johannes Kepler, whereas Jung's chapters focus on how natural laws and inexplicable coincidences (especially *meaningful* ones in the manner of synchronicity) differ. He adds a cheeky personal anecdote from his journal on 1 April 1949:

Today is Friday. We have fish for lunch. Somebody happens to mention the custom of making an 'April fish' of someone. That same morning I made a note of an inscription which read: 'Est homo totus medius piscis ab imo.' [A man is wholly fish from middle to bottom.]

In the afternoon a former patient of mine, whom I had not seen in months, showed me some extremely impressive pictures of fish which she had painted in the meantime. In the evening I was shown a piece of embroidery with fish-like sea-monsters in it.

On the morning of 2 April, another patient, whom I had not seen for many years, told me a dream in which she stood on the shore of a lake and saw a large fish that swam straight towards her and landed at her feet.

It is, admittedly, exceedingly odd that the fish theme recurs no less than six times within twenty-four hours.

Jung began in his foreword:

I hope it will not be construed as presumption on my part if I make uncommon demands on the open-mindedness and goodwill of the reader. Not only is he expected to plunge into regions of human experience which are dark, dubious and hedged about with prejudice, but the intellectual difficulties are such as the treatment and elucidation of so abstract a subject must inevitably entail.

To what extent is something ... real? Do science and psychology clash in every way possible? When do alchemy and religion enter the picture in the case of the psyche's nature? Do we have any concrete answers at all? When can psychiatrists clearly determine the root cause of a condition, or is it simply an impossible feat?

Jung argues that space and time only became 'fixed' concepts after the concept of measurement was established; in themselves, they consist of nothing. He also goes into what now is known as the Mandela effect, where people hold different recollections of the past. The symbolic Mandala (common confusion, spelled with an 'a') represents the centredness of the human condition.

While serving in the Boer War, J.W. Dunne (*An Experiment with Time*, 1927) misread 40,000 lives as 4,000, which was stamped in his memory – and he was unaware of his error until he copied the newspaper article 15 years later. He continued to live with the delusion that his memory was correct until he dug into the archives a decade and a half later.

At the interplay of Yin and Yang, the Chinese concept of *I Ching* was a comprehensive method for grasping a situation as a whole. Jung mentions the significance of two sages, from the 12th century BC, King Wen and the Duke of Chou. The pair set out to explain the simultaneous occurrence of a psychic state with a physical process as an equivalence of meaning.

With respect to astrological positions, Jung studied the conjunction and opposition of Mars and Venus – what he considered to be the governing forces behind marriage compatibility and success. He could not find statistically relevant information within his data sets and participants. This brings him to the causality principle, where there is a necessary connection between cause and effect.

Jung further draws similarities from the Chinese psychology of holistic thinking of 'completing a total picture' to philosophers of the Middle Ages from Europe, particularly Hippocrates, who said, 'The universal principle is found even in the smallest particle, which therefore corresponds to the whole.'

Agrippa (The World Soul), in the world of alchemy, is what Jung believes to be a synonym for the collective unconscious: 'The soul of the world is a certain only thing, filling all things, bestowing all things, binding, and knitting together all things, that it might make one frame of the world...'

The World Soul (or as Jung translated, 'Anima Mundi'), in a broader sense, represents a collective, universal consciousness shared by all human beings. Jung believed that there are deep-seated, archetypal images and symbols that are part of our shared human experience.

Jung illustrated the out-of-body experience with the example of one of his patients shortly after giving birth: 'Without feeling her body and its position, she was *looking down* from a point in the ceiling and could see everything going on in the room below her: she saw herself lying in the bed, deadly pale, with closed eyes.'

AION: RESEARCHES INTO THE PHENOMENOLOGY OF THE SELF

In 1951, a year after starting work on *The Interpretation of Nature and the Psyche,* Jung published *Aion: Researches into the*

Phenomenology of the Self – one of his notable works that plays at the intersection between religion, alchemy and psychology. He detailed a deeper dive into the shadow and the fragility of human consciousness. The book also delves into the idea of historical and cultural transformations. Jung suggests that certain archetypal forces emerge during specific historical periods within the collective unconscious.

Jung introduced the term 'Aion', which refers to the timelessness and eternal aspect of the human psyche. He discussed the recurring motifs of religious and mythological symbolism, and particularly focused on the archetype of the self and its association with the collective unconscious. He discussed the astrological symbolism of the transition from the Age of Pisces to the Age of Aquarius. He interpreted this transition in both psychological and cultural terms.

> *For this reason the ancients often compared the symbol to water, a case in point being tao, where yang and yin are united. Tao is the 'valley spirit', the winding course of a river.*

The central idea of 'Aion' revolves around the concept of individuation, the process through which an individual integrates and balances their conscious and unconscious elements. Jung emphasizes the importance of understanding and integrating the archetypal aspects of the self to achieve psychological wholeness and spiritual development.

Jung drew upon many examples from Christianity, Gnosticism, alchemy and other ancient belief systems to illustrate the universal nature of the archetypes and their transformative potential. He saw alchemy as an early form of psychology, where the transmutation of base metals into gold symbolized the transformation of the individual's psyche towards higher consciousness.

Alchemy can be viewed as a symbolic representation of the process of psychological transformation. In alchemical texts, the transmutation of base metals into gold was seen as an external symbol for the inner transformation of the alchemist's psyche. Jung believed that alchemists were actually working on their own inner selves, striving for self-realization and individuation.

In Gnosticism, he saw parallels between myths and archetypes in the collective unconscious. Jung touched upon Eastern concepts, such as the idea of Atman (the individual soul) and Brahman (the universal soul) in Hinduism, to emphasize the universal nature of archetypal symbols across different cultural frameworks.

He also drew on various Greek myths and deities to exemplify archetypal patterns. For instance, he associated the god Dionysus with the archetype of the self and explored the symbolism of the Uroboros, the serpent eating its own tail, as a representation of eternal cyclicality. Jung also notes that the Uroboros can take on a mandala-like form, with a circular shape and a centre point. Mandalas are often associated with spiritual and psychological wholeness.

Significance of the Apocalypse

In *Aion*, Jung explores the concept of the apocalypse in both psychological and cultural dimensions. The term 'apocalypse' is often associated with religious beliefs about the end of the world or a final judgement. However, Jung interprets the idea of the apocalypse in a broader and more symbolic sense, suggesting that it represents a profound transformation of the individual and collective psyche.

Jung views the apocalypse as a psychological event rather than a literal catastrophe. He sees it as a process of profound inner change and renewal that occurs within the individual. This inner transformation is often initiated by a confrontation with the unconscious, particularly with the contents of the collective unconscious, which may include archetypal and shadow elements.

The apocalypse, in this sense, is a symbolic representation of the death and rebirth of the ego, leading to a more integrated and authentic self. Jung's concept of the apocalypse also relates to the integration of opposites within the individual and society. It's a confrontation with the dark, chaotic aspects of the psyche (the shadow) and the potential for integrating these aspects into a more balanced and whole self. This process of integration is essential for individuation.

Generally, the term 'apocalypse' is synonymous with 'revelation'. The word 'apokalypsis' originates from Greek, with 'kalypto' as its root, signifying 'to cover' or 'to hide', while the prefix 'apo' denotes 'away from'. In essence, 'apokalypsis' conveys the idea of removing the veil or cover, potentially unveiling hidden or concealed aspects.

From this perspective, one can contemplate that apocalyptic events or psychic content might uncover novel facets of our human nature, whether on a personal or collective level. It is as if something previously unseen is striving to come to the surface. The deeper, darker, murkier parts of the collective unconscious, perhaps?

Joseph Henderson (1903–2007), the sole analyst to have collaborated with Jung, recounted that Jung once confided in him about his affection for reading the Bible. Jung's fascination

An interview with Jung, c.1955.

with the Bible extended beyond its spiritual wisdom; he found its psychological implications equally compelling. Reading the Bible, Jung believed, provided him with profound psychological insights and a deeper understanding of the human psychc.

FINAL GOODBYES TO EMMA JUNG, AND RUTH BAILEY

Emma remained loyally by Jung's side as his scientific assistant (even after their separation) until she passed away from recurring cancer on 27 November 1955. Back in the spring of the same year, Emma had to undergo surgery, which brought her back to a state of decent health. Her family truly thought she had made a full recovery and was elated at her newfound energy.

However, this happiness was short-lived. As the visionary he was, two days before her passing, Jung recalled:

> *The illumination came from my wife, who was then mostly in a coma, and that the tremendous lighting up and release of this insight worked back upon her and was one reason that she could die such a painless and regal death.*

The period following Emma's death was challenging for Jung, and he went through a deep mourning process. However, he also experienced what he considered a form of continuation of his connection with Emma on a spiritual level.

He wrote about his encounters with the spirit of Emma in his Black Books, a collection of personal journals where he documented his inner experiences and reflections. These encounters were part of Jung's exploration of the depths of the psyche and his understanding of the collective unconscious.

Jung honourably described her as 'a Queen', even after her passing (he was said to have cried out to the heavens for months). He wrote in his journal that he felt as though he had essentially lost a part of himself, and that he was struggling to find meaning in the world without her. He even carved a stone which read, after Emma's death, 'She was the foundation of my house.'

> *The very fact that a man enters into a marriage on trial means that he is making a reservation; he wants to be sure of not burning his fingers, to risk nothing.*

> *Whoever doubts marriage in the first place cannot infringe against it; for him the legal definition is invalid because, like St. Paul, he feels himself beyond the law, on the higher plane of love.*

Emma was dedicated to her role as a nurturing mother through and through, but also took her research extremely seriously. She became a steadfast Jungian analyst during her later years and even wrote two papers, *On the Nature of the Animus* and *The Anima as an Elemental Being*.

Emma Jung was not content with the role of a passive observer in her husband's work. Instead, she became a trusted collaborator, actively engaging in both personal and professional aspects of their lives. Her influence extended beyond her role as a supportive spouse to that of a true intellectual equal after their divorce.

Her peers described her as 'modest, introverted, sensible,

talented, extremely intelligent and unassuming'. She was deeply interested in art and literature, and was an accomplished artist and writer in her own right. She said, as a proud Sensing personality type who deals best with practical, tangible matters: 'I would prefer to think that one should not dream at all, one should live.'

Emma also co-authored *The Grail Legend* with Marie-Louise von Franz, which is an illustration of how this Celtic symbol prevails through mythology. Both ladies, as Jungian analysts, highlight how universal symbols such as the Wise Old Man, Virgin, Loathly

Carl with his ex-wife and research partner Emma Jung, c.1955.

Damsel, and Fool reflect upon modern societal issues. She worked on the piece for 30 years, until her passing in 1955.

She remarked, 'In our time, when such threatening forces of cleavage are at work, splitting peoples, individuals and atoms, it is doubly necessary that those which unite and hold together should become effective; for life is founded on the harmonious interplay of masculine and feminine forces, within the individual human being as well as without. Bringing these opposites into union is one of the most important tasks of present-day psychotherapy.'

In the Freud–Jung letters, Emma sadly proclaimed, 'Incidentally, America no longer has the same attraction for him [Carl] as before, and this has taken a stone from my heart.' She wanted to see her then-husband thrive as he once did while they were married, even if they were unable to work through their jarring differences.

Emma was particularly interested in the symbolism and mythology of ancient cultures, and this interest had a significant influence on her husband's work. She was also called 'dauntless' and 'enduring' as she delivered her thoughts with immense 'precision, erudition and understanding'. Jung carved the saying, 'Oh vase, sign of devotion and obedience', on her tombstone.

At times I feel as if I am spread out over the landscape and inside things, and am myself living in every tree, in the splashing of the waves, in the clouds and the animals that come and go, in the procession of the seasons.

My life has been in a sense the quintessence of what I have written, not the other way around. The way I am and the way I write are a unity. All my ideas and all my endeavours are myself. Thus the 'autobiography' is a mere dot on the 'i'.

When Jung was in his golden years, he became friends with Ruth Bailey, during the majority of the 1950s up to his death. She served as a nurse during the First World War and first met Jung accompanied by two acolytes, George Beckwith and Dr Peter Baynes. Ruth was said to have found Jung 'rude' and 'standoffish' at first. By fate or by chance, she joined Jung and his friends on their journey to Eastern Kenya and Uganda in 1925.

As their friendship developed, it is likely that Ruth's nursing background played a significant role in her relationship with Jung, especially during his later years. Jung's health declined as he aged, and having a nurse as a friend and companion proved to be valuable. Ruth's medical knowledge and care provided comfort and support to Jung in his elderly years, but she was also an integral part of his children's lives as a caretaker and a wonderful and engaging conversationalist with Jung himself. He'd remark to her, 'Your love keeps me alive,' in a genuinely platonic manner.

In turn, Ruth would have had the opportunity to engage in meaningful conversations with Jung, benefiting from his profound insights into psychology, spirituality and the human condition.

The friendship between Carl Jung and Ruth Bailey is a testament to the unpredictability and richness of human connections. What began as an encounter with initial misgivings evolved into a profound and mutually beneficial relationship that lasted until Jung's death. Their journey together and the insights they shared during this period likely left an indelible mark on both of their lives.

OLD AGE, NEW ACHIEVEMENTS AND DEATH

On 26 July 1960, his 85th birthday, Jung was named an honorary citizen of Küssnacht – one of the highest community honours of his time. That same year Jung published *Structures and Dynamics of the Psyche*, in which he proposed three parts of the psyche (or the totality of the human mind): the conscious, the personal unconscious, and the collective unconscious. Interestingly, this paper (one of his final works) became a staple in Jungian analysis later on.

The conscious is the part of the psyche that is aware of the individual's thoughts, feelings and perceptions at any given moment. It is the part of the psyche that is in direct contact with the external world and allows individuals to make decisions, solve problems and interact with others. It's the most visible and accessible part of the psyche, and can be easily observed through introspection or psychotherapy.

In contrast, the personal unconscious contains repressed or forgotten memories, as well as emotions and experiences that have not yet been fully integrated into the conscious mind. These may include childhood memories, traumatic experiences, or unexpressed feelings. The personal unconscious is not directly accessible to the conscious mind but can be accessed through techniques such as dream analysis or hypnosis.

Finally, the deepest and most mysterious part of the psyche – the collective unconscious – is a universal repository of shared, inherited experiences and symbols that are common to all humans, regardless of culture or individual experience. This includes archetypes, which are universal patterns of behaviour, thought and emotion that are inherited from our ancestors and are present in everyone.

Carl Jung and Ruth Bailey, his close friend and caregiver.

An old man who cannot bid farewell to life appears as feeble and sickly as a young man who is unable to embrace it ... it is in many cases a question of the self, same childish greediness, the same fear, the same defiance and wilfulness, in the one as in the other.

I feel that my life has been a long and winding journey, full of twists and turns that I could never have predicted. But through it all, I have tried to remain true to myself and to my inner vision.

Shortly before his passing, Jung acknowledged Mountain Lake's insight that the consciousness and significance of his people would wither away due to the stifling influence of American rationalism (cited in Berger & Segaller, 2000, p. 153).

This statement suggests that Jung believed that American society, as a collective, prioritized the thinking function at the expense of the feeling function. Within the framework of Jungian analysis, an individual exhibiting such an imbalance would be encouraged to explore ways of reconnecting with their emotional and feeling aspects (Duran, 2006).

Jung died on 6 June 1961 on the shores of Lake Zurich, Switzerland at the ripe old age of 85, just a month before his 86th birthday. He suffered an embolism during the previous month, which had impaired his speech. It was a terrifying yet eye-opening experience for Jung, who questioned his life choices and sunk into a deep well of depression. His close friend Ruth Bailey noted that shortly afterwards while they were having tea, Jung collapsed – and that was the final time he'd been spotted in the library.

People who had passed by Jung's peaceful and picturesque villa often saw him sitting on his lawn, watching his grandchildren play. He was survived by his five children – Franz, Agathe, Gret, Marianne and Helene – nineteen grandchildren, and nine great-grandchildren.

To this day, this Latin inscription is carved on the door to his Küssnacht home: *Vocatus atqua non vocatus deus aderit.* (Translation: Called or not called, God is present.) This inscription reflects Jung's belief in the presence of the divine or the transcendent in human life, regardless of whether one actively seeks or acknowledges it. His previous journeys and papers urge individuals to seek spirituality to go through the stages of life with hope and courage.

Jung's stage of Old Age serves as the crowning chapter in his psychological narrative, depicting the culmination of a lifelong odyssey towards self-realization. As individuals navigate the twilight of their years, Jung illuminates the transformative potential inherent in embracing the archetypal dimensions of the unconscious.

The integration of life's experiences, the reconciliation of opposites, and the cultivation of wisdom become paramount in this final stage. Old Age, according to Jung, offers the opportunity for a profound understanding of the self and an intimate connection to the collective unconscious.

CHAPTER 6

THE RIPPLING EFFECT OF JUNG'S LEGACY

Carl Jung pioneered the field of analytic psychology and shook the world of psychiatry through his dream analysis process and archetype identification. Certain theories are far-fetched and even outlandish – deemed 'overly complex', 'untranslatable' and even 'gibberish' by some. Jung's work has always been a hot topic of debate within the psychiatric community, love or hate him.

His magnetic influence sparked the birth of various organizations that focus on his research and apply them to modern-day issues. From industrial organizational growth to personal development, there's a Jungian concept that can help foster understanding and bridge the gap between psychological theory and application.

C.G. Jung Institute: The C.G. Jung Institute is an international organization with numerous regional and local branches. These institutes offer training and education in analytical psychology and promote the continued study and application of Jung's ideas. The C.G. Jung Institute in Zurich, where Jung himself worked, is particularly well known.

International Association for Analytical Psychology (IAAP): IAAP is an organization that connects Jungian analysts and institutions worldwide. It supports the development of analytical psychology, organizes conferences and fosters collaboration among those interested in Jung's work.

The Philemon Foundation: This organization is dedicated to the publication and preservation of Carl Jung's unpublished works and *The Red Book*, a personal journal and work of art that Jung kept during a period of personal crisis. Their efforts help make Jung's less-known writings more accessible to the public.

Notable figures Jung has influenced include psychologists Abraham Maslow and Carl Rogers, as well as physicist Wolfgang Pauli. Jung had a vision for his work to inspire people to figure out who they really are; to take a lifelong journey to fulfil their mission to confront their shadow and undergo metamorphosis to emerge as their highest, most individuated self.

As Jung proudly announced to the world: 'The privilege of a lifetime is to become who you truly are.' We all have the opportunity to shine a light on our shadows and accept all parts of ourselves as valid and important. Imagine how chaotic and self-destructive a society would be if every person shared the same personality preferences!

NEO-JUNGIAN PERSONALITY ASSESSMENTS

From psychometric testing such as the 16PFQ (16 Personality Factor Questionnaire) to the MMPI (Minnesota Multiphasic Personality Inventory) to the MBTI® (Myers–Briggs Type Indicator), Jung's teachings reach far and wide. His work has been reintroduced to the world through therapy, personality assessments and art both on paper and the big screen.

MBTI®

The MBTI® incorporates additional elements such as the concept of preferences, the 16 personality types and practical applications in career counselling, team-building and personal development. Although it is considered to teeter on the side of pseudoscience, it can be a helpful and insightful tool in self-discovery and reflection. It can also help fiction writers formulate complex, interesting characters and captivating plots.

Almost every postsecondary psychology course will have a section specifically on his work because of how tremendously influential it has been to the field. Jung's work has also profoundly influenced the fields of child development, literature, philosophy, religion, and even archaeology. Look into any subject Jung himself studied in the past – and discover the many echoes of his voice that remain.

Jung's book *Psychological Types* laid the groundwork for the MBTI® (Myers–Briggs Type Indicator). He proposed that individuals have innate preferences for how they perceive and judge information, which he classified into eight cognitive functions (four perceiving and four judging functions).

The world-famous MBTI® was the result of the collaboration between a mother–daughter duo, Katharine Cook Briggs (1875–1968) and Isabel Briggs Myers (1897–1980). Their approach differed from that of Jung, as they believed personality reflected inherent abilities (fixed mindset), while Jung focused on preferences.

Katharine Cook Briggs delved into Jung's theory of personality types in 1923 and found it highly enlightening. In 1926, she penned a lengthy and descriptive essay on child-rearing titled *Meet Yourself Using the Personality Paint Box*. The papers consist of multiple elements from Ms Briggs: two scrapbooks, three folders containing genealogical materials, and a selection of both public and personal writings.

During the same year, she also developed a basic questionnaire based on Jung's theory to evaluate personality types. Over the next several years, Katharine and Jung exchanged numerous letters until she convinced him to meet in person in the United States in 1937. And so their cordial yet highly theoretical discussions on the classification of human nature began.

This formed the basis for the four dichotomies used in the MBTI®:

1. **Extraversion (E) vs. Introversion (I)** – How people gain energy
2. **Sensing (S) vs. Intuition (N)** – How people gather information
3. **Thinking (T) vs. Feeling (F)** – How people make decisions
4. **Judging (J) vs. Perceiving (P)** – How people organize their environment and time

There are multiple versions of the indicator:

1. **Original MBTI®:** The original MBTI® was developed by Katharine Cook Briggs and her daughter Isabel in the mid-20th century. It was based on Jung's theory of personality types and focused on the four dichotomies listed above.
2. **MBTI® Step I:** This is the most common and widely used version of the MBTI®. It consists of a self-report questionnaire that assesses personality preferences based

Katharine Cook Briggs and Isabel Briggs Myers, the mother daughter duo behind the MBTI®.

on the four dichotomies. It provides individuals with a four-letter personality type code (e.g., INFJ or ESTP).

3. **MBTI® Step II**: MBTI® Step II is a more comprehensive version of the assessment that provides a more detailed and nuanced understanding of personality. It breaks down each of the four dichotomies into facets, resulting in a more complex and personalized profile.

4. **Form M and Form Q**: These are different forms or versions of the MBTI® questionnaire. Form M is the most commonly used, while Form Q includes additional questions and is sometimes used for research purposes.

5. **MBTI® Type Table**: Some adaptations of the MBTI® use a type table format, which presents the 16 personality types in a matrix that shows how the types are related to each other.

6. **Online Versions**: With the advent of online personality tests, many websites and platforms offer free or paid versions of the MBTI® assessment. These digital versions often provide immediate results and interpretations.

7. **Adaptations for Specific Populations**: There have been adaptations of the MBTI® for specific purposes or populations, such as the 'Strong Interest Inventory' for career counselling and the 'Murphy–Meisgeier Type Indicator for Children®' for assessing personality in children.

8. **MBTI® in Various Languages**: The MBTI® has been translated into multiple languages to make it accessible to a global audience. These translations aim to maintain the integrity of the assessment while accommodating linguistic and cultural differences.

The MBTI® takes these preferences into account and generates a four-letter personality type (e.g., ISTJ, ENFP) that represents an individual's dominant preferences across these dimensions. This totals up to 16 personality type possibilities, each with their own strengths, weaknesses and career suggestions.

For example, someone who tests as an ESFJ (purported to be the most common personality type in the world) would gain energy from being around others, gather information through their senses, make decisions based on their feelings, and prefer to have clear-cut deadlines when they organize their time.

The opposite personality would be the INTP, who would instead gain energy from being alone, gather information through inference, make decisions based on logic, and prefer to keep plans open-ended in case more intriguing opportunities arise. Quite different people, indeed! These two personality types may clash in some ways, and be able to help each other grow in others.

However, this simplification comes at a cost. Jung's original theory was a nuanced and complex exploration of the human psyche, recognizing that individuals are not easily pigeonholed into fixed categories. He emphasized the dynamic and fluid nature of personality, acknowledging that people can exhibit a range of behaviours and characteristics depending on various factors such as context, development and life experiences.

Moreover, the MBTI® is a self-report assessment, meaning that individuals answer a series of questions about their preferences, and the assessment categorizes them based on their responses. This self-report nature introduces several potential limitations, and as previously mentioned, is highly reductionistic and should be seen as a tool instead of a be-all, end-all doctrine.

People may not always accurately assess their own preferences due to biases, self-perception issues, or the desire to present themselves in a certain way. Additionally, the binary nature of the MBTI® (you're either an Extravert or an Introvert, for instance) doesn't happen to capture the full, colourful spectrum of human personality variations.

Furthermore, the MBTI® doesn't account for other important factors in personality, such as individual differences, cultural influences, or the impact of life experiences. It's a somewhat static model that doesn't accommodate the complexities of human development and growth over time.

In contrast, Jung's original theory allowed for a more holistic and flexible understanding of personality. It emphasized the importance of balancing and integrating different aspects of one's personality to achieve individuation, a process of becoming one's true self. Jung's work also delved into the depths of the unconscious mind and explored archetypes and symbols, providing a broader context for understanding the human psyche.

While the MBTI® extends upon Jung's original framework, it simplifies and operationalizes his ideas into a practical and accessible tool for understanding personality. It is critical to note that the MBTI® is a self-report assessment and does not fully capture the sheer complexity of Jung's original theory.

Psychometricians today strongly warn against using the MBTI® for hiring purposes, although the Briggs–Myers mother–daughter duo started off by profiling people for job–personality fit. The assessment is now commonly used for career counselling, team-building exercises and personal development.

The Keirsey Temperament Sorter

In 1956, American psychologist David Keirsey (1921–2013) devised the Keirsey Temperament Sorter. Keirsey's interest in personality psychology was sparked after the Second World War when he delved into the writings of William Sheldon and Ernst Kretschmer. He earned his PhD in counselling psychology from Claremont Graduate University.

Drawing inspiration from Hippocrates' four humours, Keirsey transformed them into his own Temperament Sorter, comprising the Artisan, Guardian, Idealist and Rational types. These temperaments loosely corresponded to the personality categories of Sensing–Perceiving (SP), Sensing–Judging (SJ), Intuitive–Feeling (NF), and Intuitive–Thinking (NT):

- Artisans (SP): Artisans are spontaneous, action-oriented and enjoy living in the present moment. They value freedom, excitement and flexibility. They are often seen as the 'Creators' and 'Adventurers'.
- Guardians (SJ): Guardians are known for their strong sense of duty, responsibility and order. They value tradition, stability and tend to be practical and dependable. They are often seen as the 'Protectors' of society.
- Idealists (NF): Idealists are empathetic, imaginative and value personal growth and meaningful connections with others. They are often motivated by a desire to make the world a better place and are seen as the 'Counsellors' and 'Healers'.
- Rationals (NT): Rationals are logical, analytical and value knowledge and competence. They seek understanding and

solutions to complex problems. They are often seen as the 'Intellectuals' and 'Strategists'.

While Keirsey's temperaments were influenced by Jung's psychological types, Keirsey's approach focused more on observable behaviours and practical applications. He aimed to create a system that could be easily understood and applied in everyday life, including areas such as career choices, relationships and personal development.

Variations and updates to the Keirsey Temperament Sorter (KTS) have been developed over the years to refine and expand upon the original model. These adaptations aim to address some of the limitations of the original KTS and provide a more nuanced understanding of personality. Here's a deep dive into some of the notable variations and updates:

The original KTS vaguely corresponded with the Myers–Briggs Type Indicator (MBTI®) in terms of the four temperaments. Both systems used the same four temperaments – Artisans, Guardians, Idealists and Rationals – though the specific names and descriptions of the temperaments may vary slightly between the two systems. David Keirsey's work was influenced by his early exposure to the MBTI®.

Keirsey authored two books, *Please Understand Me* and *Please Understand Me II*, which introduced and expanded upon the KTS. These books provided detailed descriptions of the 16 Keirsey Temperament Types and how they relate to various aspects of life, including relationships, career choices and communication styles.

In *Please Understand Me II*, Keirsey introduced the concept of 'interaction styles'. These styles describe how individuals engage with others in social situations. There are four interaction styles, which align with the four temperaments:

- Get-Things-Going (Artisans): Artisans are spontaneous and enjoy initiating interactions. They are adaptable and flexible.
- Chart-the-Course (Guardians): These individuals prefer organizing and planning interactions. They tend to be methodical and structured.
- Behind-the-Scenes (Idealists): Idealists prefer supportive roles in interactions, often providing encouragement and empathy.
- In-Charge (Rationals): Rationals take charge in interactions, often leading and directing discussions. They are focused on achieving goals.

An updated version of the KTS, known as the 'Temperament Sorter II', was introduced in *Please Understand Me II*. This version refined the descriptions of temperament traits and included more comprehensive profiles for each of the 16 personality types.

Some researchers have conducted studies to investigate the validity of the KTS and its relationship to brain activity and behaviour. These studies have explored potential correlations between temperament types and brain patterns, though the results are not universally accepted by the scientific community.

The KTS has been integrated with other personality models and frameworks, such as the Big Five Personality Traits and the Enneagram, to provide a more holistic understanding of personality. These integrations acknowledge that personality is multifaceted and cannot be fully captured by a single model.

With the advent of the internet, online versions of the KTS have become widely available. These tools allow individuals to complete the assessment and receive their temperament type online. They often include detailed personality profiles and interpretations.

The KTS, like the MBTI®, has faced criticism for its simplicity and lack of empirical support. Critics argue that it may not accurately capture the complexity of human personality. Additionally, some psychologists and researchers have raised concerns about the lack of scientific rigour in the development and validation of the KTS.

The Thematic Apperception Test

Another assessment Jung influenced is the Thematic Apperception Test (TAT), which uses ambiguous pictures to assess an individual's unconscious thoughts, feelings and motivations. It was primarily developed by American psychologists Henry A. Murray and Christiana D. Morgan in the 1930s, based on their own research and theoretical perspectives.

The TAT is rooted in the belief that when faced with ambiguous stimuli, individuals will project their own thoughts, emotions and experiences on to these stimuli, revealing aspects of their inner world that might be otherwise difficult to access through direct questioning. This concept is in line with Jung's notion of the unconscious, where deep-seated and often unacknowledged aspects of the psyche reside.

The TAT consists of a series of black-and-white pictures, typically 31 in total, including one blank card. These pictures depict a wide range of scenes and scenarios, such as interpersonal interactions, landscapes and ambiguous situations. The assessment process involves presenting individuals with a series of these ambiguous pictures and asking them to create a story based on each image. Participants are encouraged to describe what they believe is happening in the picture, including the thoughts, emotions and motivations of the characters depicted. These narratives are then analysed to gain insights into the individual's perceptions, concerns and motivations – allowing for the assessment of underlying psychological themes and dynamics.

Recurring themes or motifs in an individual's narratives may reflect the presence of certain archetypes, such as the hero, the trickster and the anima or animus. Symbolic elements within the stories may also hold meaning and provide insights into the individual's unconscious processes.

The TAT is considered a projective test because it relies on the idea that individuals will project their unconscious thoughts, emotions and conflicts on to the ambiguous images, providing insights into their inner world. The stories they create are believed to reveal aspects of their personality, including their needs, fears, wishes and conflicts.

The test is typically administered individually by a trained psychologist or clinician. The test-taker is presented with one card at a time and their responses are recorded and later analysed.

Scoring the TAT involves examining various elements of the stories, including:

- Themes: Analysts identify recurring themes, motifs and patterns in the stories, such as themes related to power, intimacy, achievement or conflict.
- Characters: The characters in the stories, their roles

and relationships are analysed to gain insight into the individual's interpersonal dynamics.

- Emotions: The emotional content of the stories, including the expressed feelings of the characters and the individual's own emotional responses, is assessed.
- Conflict Resolution: How the characters in the stories resolve conflicts and challenges can provide insights into the individual's coping mechanisms and problem-solving strategies.

Various branches of psychology implement the TAT, including clinical psychology, research and organizational psychology. Some common applications include:

- Psychological Assessment: In clinical settings, the TAT can help clinicians understand a patient's underlying psychological issues, such as trauma, personality disorders or unresolved conflicts.
- Personality Research: Researchers use the TAT to investigate personality traits, motivations and emotional patterns in different populations.
- Organizational Psychology: Some organizations use projective tests like the TAT in employee assessments to gain insights into an individual's work-related values and motivations.

While the TAT has been a valuable tool in psychology, it also has its limitations and criticisms:

- Subjectivity: Scoring the TAT relies on the interpretation of the analyst, which can introduce subjectivity and variability in results.
- Reliability and Validity: Some researchers have questioned the reliability and validity of the TAT as a measure of personality traits.
- Cultural Bias: The images and scenarios in the TAT may not be equally relevant or meaningful across different cultures, potentially introducing cultural bias.

Overall, the Thematic Apperception Test is a valuable tool for psychologists and therapists to gain a deeper understanding of an individual's inner world. Its roots in Jungian psychology, with a focus on archetypal themes and symbolism, allow it to tap into the rich tapestry of the unconscious mind and provide insights into an individual's thoughts, emotions and motivations that may be hidden from conscious awareness.

ENTERTAINMENT AND POPULAR CULTURE

Jung on the Big Screen

Carl Jung's archetypal theories and ideas about personality development have left an indelible mark on the world of modern arts and entertainment. From the grandeur of the Star Wars and Harry Potter series to the subtlety of Broadway plays and the chilling depths of horror titles, echoes of Jung's intellectual legacy can be discovered hidden almost everywhere in these creative realms.

One of the most notable manifestations of Jung's influence is seen in the hero's journey, a narrative structure deeply rooted in

Jungian archetypes. Epitomized by characters like Frodo Baggins in *The Lord of the Rings*, this archetype guides protagonists through transformative journeys, mirroring the universal human experience of facing challenges, confronting inner demons, and emerging as changed individuals.

The shadow archetype, representing the darker aspects of the human psyche, finds a home in the horror genre. It materializes fears and anxieties as grotesque monsters or malevolent forces, as exemplified in Stephen King's *It*. This use of the shadow archetype allows horror creators to tap into the deep-seated fears of their audiences, making the experience all the more psychologically chilling.

In the mentorship of characters like Obi-Wan Kenobi in *Star Wars* or Gandalf in *The Hobbit*, the Mentor archetype emerges, embodying wisdom and guidance. These mentors, reminiscent of Jung's wise old man archetype, help heroes navigate their paths to self-discovery, echoing Jung's belief in the importance of guidance and mentorship in the journey towards individuation.

Jung's concept of the anima and animus, representing the feminine and masculine aspects within individuals, often forms the basis of complex character relationships. In romance stories, such as Disney's *Beauty and the Beast*, the tension and growth between characters reflect the interplay of these archetypal forces and the journey towards mutual understanding.

The Trickster archetype, characterized by characters like Loki in the Marvel Cinematic Universe or the Mad Hatter in *Alice in Wonderland*, challenges norms and disrupts the status quo. These figures serve as sources of comic relief and encourage reflection on societal conventions, aligning with Jung's idea of the Trickster as a catalyst for change and transformation.

Beyond character archetypes, Jung's ideas also influence symbols and motifs. Concepts like rebirth and transformation, symbolized by the phoenix or the lotus flower, recur in various films and literature, representing personal growth and renewal.

Phoenix symbols have appeared in popular movies like *Harry Potter and the Order of the Phoenix*, *X-Men: The Last Stand* and *Fantastic Beasts and Where to Find Them*. The lotus flower can be found in *American Beauty*, *The Little Buddha*, and *The Matrix Revolutions*.

In essence, Carl Jung's archetypal theories continue to serve as a profound wellspring of inspiration for storytellers across diverse mediums. They provide a framework for crafting characters and narratives that resonate with the complexities of the human experience.

Movie by Movie

In literature, countless authors have incorporated archetypal figures and narratives in their works. J.R.R. Tolkien's *The Lord of the Rings* features archetypal heroes on a mythical quest, while George Lucas drew heavily from Jungian archetypes in creating the iconic characters in the *Star Wars* saga.

Jung's influence extends to films like *The Matrix*, where the hero's journey and the concept of self-realization are central themes. *The Matrix* follows the classic hero's journey, a storytelling framework that was studied and popularized by the American writer Joseph Campbell, who had connections to Jungian psychology.

Neo, the protagonist, undergoes a transformation from an ordinary individual to a hero who must confront and integrate his shadow (the darker, hidden aspects of his psyche) in order to fulfil his destiny.

Jungian psychology introduced the concept of archetypes, universal symbols and themes found in the collective unconscious of humanity. *The Matrix* includes archetypal characters such as the wise mentor (Morpheus), the hero (Neo), the villain (Agent Smith), and the oracle, each embodying various archetypal elements.

The concept of the shadow, a hidden and often repressed part of the individual's psyche, is central in Jungian psychology. Neo confronts his own shadow when he meets Agent Smith, a formidable antagonist who represents a dark, negative aspect of his own psyche. The battle between Neo and Agent Smith can be seen as a psychological struggle between the ego and the shadow.

Jung's theory of individuation is the process of integrating the various aspects of one's personality and becoming a more whole and authentic self. Neo's journey can be interpreted as a journey of individuation, as he seeks to understand and integrate the different aspects of himself and transcend the limitations of the artificial world.

The choice offered to Neo, represented by the red pill and the blue pill, can be seen as a symbolic representation of the individual's choice to awaken a deeper, more authentic reality (red pill) or remain in a comfortable, illusory world (blue pill). This choice parallels the process of self-discovery and awakening often associated with Jungian psychology.

Films like Christopher Nolan's *Inception* delve into the realm of dreams, exploring their power, symbolism and the unconscious desires they may reveal. Jung's concept of the shadow, representing the darker, repressed aspects of the self, is often explored in horror movies. Here, monsters and villains become symbolic manifestations of these hidden aspects.

In the film, Cobb's guilt and unresolved issues with his late wife, Mal, are central to the plot. The dream world becomes a metaphor for Cobb's inner journey to confront his shadow and unresolved psychological conflicts. Jung would argue that this exploration of the shadow is essential for personal growth and integration.

Donnie Darko has a frightening rabbit antagonist named Frank that symbolizes the main character's underlying (and largely subconscious) fears. Frank, a haunting and nightmarish figure who appears to Donnie in a rabbit suit, can be seen as Donnie's shadow.

In Jungian psychology, the shadow, again, represents the darker, hidden aspects of the self. Frank's presence serves as a manifestation of Donnie's repressed fears, desires and destructive tendencies. He frantically tries to run away from Frank, but the rabbit's power grows the more he fears him.

Donnie wears a mask of the troubled teenager to conform to societal norms, concealing his deeper struggles and emotions. Jungian psychology would suggest that Donnie's mask is his persona, and his journey involves removing this mask to reveal his authentic self.

The film presents archetypal characters and situations, such as the wise old man (Donnie's therapist, Dr Thurman), the Trickster (Frank), and the hero's journey. These archetypal elements are central to Donnie's psychological development and the unfolding of the plot.

The film features several instances of synchronicity, which Jung believed to be meaningful coincidences that reflect a connection between the inner and outer worlds. The mysterious events in the film, such as the jet engine crash and the time travel elements, can be seen as examples of synchronicity, signalling the alignment of Donnie's inner world with external events.

Donnie's experiences with time travel and the manipulation of reality can be seen as a journey into the collective unconscious, where he encounters symbolic and mythological elements that are shared by all of humanity. The thin fabric of reality that separates his dream world and the tangible world almost blends together at various points in the story.

The process of individuation, which Jung described as the realization of one's true self, is central to the film. Donnie's journey can be interpreted as a quest for self-discovery and integration. His encounters with various characters and his experiences with time manipulation lead him to a deeper understanding of himself and his purpose.

The Red Shoes is a classic film about the conflict between artistic passion and personal identity. It explores the archetype of the 'dancing woman' and the idea of the artist's journey as a path of self-discovery.

The red ballet shoes in the film can be seen as a symbol of the protagonist's shadow self, which is a central concept in Jung's psychology. The shadow represents the repressed or hidden aspects of one's personality.

In the film, the shoes become an obsession for the protagonist, Vicky Page, and they drive her to the brink of madness. This obsession with the red shoes can be seen as an externalization of her own repressed desires and darker aspects of her psyche.

A Beautiful Mind is based on the life of mathematician John Nash, and deals with the theme of psychological transformation and the integration of the shadow self. Nash's struggle with schizophrenia is portrayed as a journey towards self-acceptance.

The psychological thriller *Black Swan* examines the descent into madness and the pursuit of perfection. The protagonist's transformation and confrontation with her dark side reflect Jungian concepts of the shadow self.

Jungian Archetypes on TV

Jungian archetypes can also be found in several television shows. *Legion*, for example, follows the story of David Haller, a mutant with powerful psychic abilities. The show incorporates elements of surrealism and explores the fragmented nature of the main character psyche.

Legion draws heavily from Jungian ideas, including the exploration of the unconscious and the integration of different aspects of the self. For example, the character of the shadow, often an antagonist representing repressed aspects of the self, is prominent in the show. Characters like the wise mentor (Melanie Bird) and the hero's journey are elements commonly found in stories that reflect Jungian archetypes.

Another show with Jung's influences is *Hannibal*, a psychological thriller series that explores the complex relationship between FBI profiler Will Graham and cannibalistic serial killer Hannibal Lecter. It delves into the dark depths of the human psyche, exploring Jungian concepts such as the shadow and the often perplexingly complex nature of evil.

Music – The Language of the Soul

To begin the Jungian setlist, play 'Imagine' by John Lennon. This iconic song envisions a world without divisions and encourages listeners to imagine a better, more unified society, reflecting Jungian ideas of collective consciousness and unity – a wholeness and peace achieved through integration and harmony.

'Imagine there's no heaven / It's easy if you try':
This line suggests an exploration of the idea of transcending traditional religious beliefs or constructs. In Jungian terms, it can be seen as an invitation to look beyond the collective conscious representations of divinity (heaven) and find a more personal, individuated understanding of spirituality.

'No hell below us / Above us only sky':
Here, the notion of a world without punishment or retribution (hell) is proposed, and the sky as a symbol of limitless possibilities is introduced. From a Jungian perspective, this could symbolize the liberation of one's psyche from fear, guilt or external judgement, and the embrace of personal growth and potential.

'Imagine all the people / Living for today':
This line implies a focus on the present moment, which aligns with Jung's emphasis on individuation and the process of becoming one's true self. Living in the present and exploring one's inner world can lead to self-discovery and growth.

'Imagine there's no countries / It isn't hard to do':
The idea of a world without borders or divisions may be seen as a call for the recognition of a shared human identity. In a Jungian context, it could be interpreted as transcending the ego's identification with specific national or cultural identities and recognizing a deeper, collective human identity.

'Nothing to kill or die for / And no religion too':
This line reflects a desire for a world free from the conflicts and divisions

often fuelled by ideology and religion. From a Jungian perspective, it could symbolize the need to transcend rigid belief systems and dogma, allowing individuals to explore their own spiritual paths and values.

'You may say I'm a dreamer / But I'm not the only one': This line acknowledges the dreamer's vision of a more harmonious world and suggests that others share this dream. It aligns with Jung's idea of archetypes and collective unconscious elements that resonate with shared human experiences and aspirations.

In 'Imagine', John Lennon's lyrics convey a vision of a world free from strife and division, where individuals can reach their full potential and live in harmony.

David Bowie, a legendary musician and performer, was deeply influenced by Jungian psychology. In his album *The Man Who Sold the World*, the song 'The Supermen' references Nietzsche and explores the idea of powerful, god-like figures. Bowie's alter ego, Ziggy Stardust, can be seen as an embodiment of the concept of the highly fluid and androgynous anima and animus.

Tool, an alternative metal band, often explore Jung's concepts in their music. In their album *Lateralus*, the song 'Schism' delves into the themes of division and integration, reflecting Jung's concept of the union of opposites. The band's lyrics frequently touch on themes of self-awareness, transformation and the exploration of the unconscious. 'Third Eye' is another song by Tool that explores themes of enlightenment, perception and inner exploration, which align with Jungian concepts of self-discovery.

'Black Hole Sun' by Soundgarden explores themes of despair and inner darkness, reflecting Jungian concepts of the shadow self and the need to confront one's inner demons.

Florence Welch, the lead vocalist of Florence + The Machine, has expressed an interest in Jungian psychology. In her album *Lungs*, the song 'Rabbit Heart (Raise It Up)' touches on themes of transformation and the shadow aspect of the self. Welch's lyrical exploration of themes like duality, darkness and the quest for self-acceptance aligns with Jung's ideas of integrating the unconscious. She sings, 'I must become a lion hearted girl / Ready for a fight / Before I make the final sacrifice.' The song's title evokes the archetype of the rabbit, which can symbolize vulnerability, fear or a desire for escape. Jung often discussed the concept of archetypes, universal symbols and themes found in the human psyche. The rabbit may represent a part of the singer's psyche that needs to be protected or nurtured.

While many stories follow the hero's journey archetype, Jungian analyst Maureen Murdock proposed the heroine's journey, which focuses on the female experience. In the Florence + The Machine song, there may be elements of the heroine's journey where the protagonist faces challenges and undergoes transformation. Jung also emphasized the importance of integrating the shadow, the darker and less known aspects of one's psyche. In the song, the lyrics could be seen as the protagonist's struggle to confront and integrate these shadow elements.

Video Games Etched with Jung

Many video game narratives follow the hero's journey, mirroring the stages of individuation and personal growth outlined by Jung. Games like *The Legend of Zelda* series, *Silent Hill* and *Bioshock Infinite* incorporate archetypal characters, mythical elements and psychological themes, engaging players in quests for self-discovery and transformation.

Some entries in *The Legend of Zelda* franchise, such as 'Ocarina of Time' and 'Majora's Mask', have been discussed in relation to Jungian concepts. These games involve journeys of self-discovery, the exploration of archetypal characters, and the hero's quest to overcome their inner and external challenges.

In *Bioshock Infinite*, the first-person shooter incorporates themes of choice, identity and parallel realities (universes). The player delves into rebellion and revolution with the 'Vox Populi', a group of rebels fighting against the oppressive ruling class. This struggle represents the clash between society and the individual's own internal conflicts, akin to Jung's concept of the collective unconscious and the shadow archetype.

Dark Souls is known for its deep lore and complex, atmospheric world. The games are replete with symbolism and themes of struggle, perseverance and self-discovery. The narrative is often cryptic, inviting players to interpret its deeper meanings. *Dark Souls* features a variety of characters, both allies and enemies, who embody Jungian archetypes.

For example, Solaire of Astora embodies the archetype of the hero, striving to fulfil a heroic quest against insurmountable odds. Gwyn, Lord of Cinder, represents the wise old man archetype, while characters like Artorias embody the shadow archetype, representing the darker aspects of the self.

The conflict between light and dark is a central theme in the *Dark Souls* series, echoing the Jungian concept of the struggle between the conscious and unconscious aspects of the psyche. Characters like Manus and the Abyss exemplify the chaos and darkness lurking in the collective unconscious, while the linking of the First Flame represents an attempt to bring light and order to the world.

The bestselling Japanese action role-playing game *NieR: Automata* explores the nature of humanity and consciousness through the experiences of androids and machines. The game delves into existential questions and features characters that can be interpreted as archetypal, such as the infamous female heroine protagonist 2B and her aggressive shadow, A2.

One of the central themes in the game is the duality of human and machine. This duality can be seen as a reflection of Carl Jung's concept of opposites and the need for balance. In the game, both the androids and the machines struggle with their dual nature, and the characters often have to confront their own inner conflicts and contradictions.

NieR incorporates various mythological and symbolic elements. For example, the concept of the Tower, a recurring motif, can be associated with the Tower card in tarot, symbolizing destruction and renewal. Jungian analysis often involves interpreting symbols to understand their psychological significance.

The game explores the collective unconscious, as seen in the shared memories and experiences of the androids. This shared consciousness parallels Jung's idea of a collective unconscious that contains universal symbols and archetypes. The androids in the game exhibit emotions, forming connections with each other and the players.

The cyclical nature of the game, with its multiple playthroughs and recurring events, reflects the idea of eternal return. This repetition contributes to the sense of a collective journey experienced by different characters. The repetition of certain events across playthroughs mirrors the recurrence of archetypal motifs found in the collective unconscious.

Jung's theory of the anima and animus suggests that individuals have both masculine and feminine aspects within them. In *NieR:*

Automata, main characters like 2B and 9S have elements of both genders, which can be seen as a reflection of the anima and animus archetypes. Heroine 2B embodies many masculine traits, whereas 9S has a healthy balance of the feminine.

The journeys of these two characters can be viewed as a process of individuation. Through their memories, they confront their own inner conflicts and strive for self-realization. 2B, initially perceived as a stoic and duty-first heroine, eventually develops empathy for other machine lifeforms and reveals a softer side.

9S, in contrast, started off more whimsical and free-wheeling. He stammered over his words, and desperately sought the approval of his teammate, 2B. After her death, he had to put his morals in question as an android – and decided to carry through their mission, 'For the glory of mankind.'

In Jungian psychology, there is an emphasis on the division between the conscious and unconscious mind. *The Stanley Parable* plays with this division by challenging the player's understanding of reality.

The player must make various choices that will determine their fate, whether that's being stuck in an echo chamber filled with computer screens or in a wonky parallel dimension. The narrator gives instructions on where to go (e.g. the door on your left, down the hall). The player then has an illusion of free will where they can choose to accept or ignore his suggestions.

The game explores the idea that our conscious choices are influenced by underlying unconscious factors, much like the hidden narratives and endings in the game that influence the player's decisions. The central theme of choice and free will in *The Stanley Parable* is reminiscent of Jung's ideas about the tension between the conscious and unconscious, as well as the struggle for individuation and true agency.

Jung believed in universal archetypes in human culture and storytelling. *The Stanley Parable* features archetypal characters and scenarios that players encounter, such as the narrator, who represents the voice of authority, and the various narrative paths that can be seen as embodying different archetypal journeys.

Players can make choices that lead to different narrative paths and endings, effectively exploring the consequences of those choices. This mirrors the idea of individuation, where one's choices shape personal development. The game's various endings and scenarios tap into archetypal situations, reflecting universal themes and patterns.

The game also hints at the concept of the shadow, a central idea in Jungian psychology. The player's choices can lead to both light-hearted and dark outcomes, reflecting the dual nature of the human psyche. The game encourages players to confront and explore these different aspects of themselves through their choices.

It calls into question the nature of the game world, the narrator's authority, and the player's control, which can be seen as a reflection of Jungian ideas regarding the subjective nature of reality and the influence of the unconscious on our perceptions.

ART THERAPY WITH JUNG'S PAINTBRUSH

Jung's work also had a tremendous influence on art therapy. He wanted people to embrace their artistic impulses and garner a sense of creative freedom. As an avid promoter of mixed media, Jung encouraged each artist to consider elements of colour, placement, content and materials in a piece. The artistic alchemy between the psyche and reality – through pen, paintbrush or moulding. The transcendence of feeling and art.

Jung's emphasis on the integration of opposites and the reconciliation of conflicts is also relevant in art therapy. Through the artistic process, individuals can explore and reconcile conflicting emotions, desires and aspects of their personality. Art therapists trained in Jungian approaches help clients make connections between their artistic expressions and their rich inner experiences.

Art is a kind of innate drive that seizes a human being and makes him its instrument. The artist is not a person endowed with free will who seeks his own ends, but one who allows art to realize its purpose through him.

In art therapy, active imagination is facilitated through art-making. Clients are encouraged to enter into a dialogue with their artwork, allowing images to unfold and speak to them. Through this process, the individual gains insights, resolves conflicts and integrates aspects of their psyche.

Art therapists deploy various art materials, such as paint, clay and collage, to facilitate active imagination and provide a tangible representation of the inner world. As an individual, the artist is subject to the vicissitudes of moods, possesses an autonomous will and pursues personal objectives.

Creativity, in this context, is articulated as the capacity to elucidate visionary metaphorical connections, surpassing mere psychological interconnections. Art has the potential to transcend idiosyncratic experiences and resonate with the profound recesses of the artist – and ultimately establish a connection with the collective unconscious of humanity.

When patients who undergo art therapy create their masterpieces through a Jungian lens, they have the opportunity to channel their libido, which Jung professed to be a general psychic energy (as opposed to Sigmund Freud's exclusively sexual view). This energy encompasses psychological and emotional energy rather than just sexual energy. It's the driving force behind desires, passions and creative impulses.

This helps reduce the conflict between their clashing forces of internal and external energy. A large amount of the libido is stored in the unconscious, so art therapy can essentially help people understand their hidden or repressed emotions. The range of different shades Jung's paint palette holds represents the many feelings that every individual can feel. Essentially, everyone is an artist in their own right.

CONCLUSION

Some psychiatrists are proudly self-proclaimed 'Jungian analysts' whose work extends upon Jung's teachings. Now in the 21st century, there exists countless organizations and clubs for Jungian enthusiasts, such as the International Association for Jungian Studies (IAJS). Their goal is to effectively implement instinctual motivation coupled with love and power to facilitate healthy self-growth in each individual.

Active imagination is a technique used in Jungian analysis that involves consciously engaging with and dialoguing with unconscious material. It allows clients to explore and give form to their inner experiences, fantasies and symbolic imagery. By actively engaging with these images and symbols, individuals can gain insights, process emotions and foster their transformation from the inside out.

Jungian analysts encourage clients to delve into dreams, fantasies and spontaneous imagery as a means of accessing and understanding hidden psychological material. Dream analysis plays a central role, as dreams are seen as a gateway to the unconscious, containing valuable symbols and messages that provide insights into the individual's psyche. Their goal is to unravel the deeper layers of their unconscious minds.

A central aim of Jungian analysis is to guide individuals on the path of individuation, a process of becoming whole and integrating all aspects of the self. Individuation involves reconciling opposites, acknowledging and integrating the shadow aspects of the personality, and developing a conscious relationship with the anima (the feminine aspects in men) or animus (the masculine aspects in women).

This process is also known as shadow work – clients explore their shadow self, which represents the hidden or repressed aspects of their personality. Through discussion and introspection, clients can work to integrate these aspects into their conscious awareness. When someone makes amends with their shadow, only then can they understand their deep-seated triggers.

Carl Jung's *Red Book* is a personal journal filled with elaborate artwork and text. Clients may be encouraged to keep their own version of a 'Red Book' as a means of exploring their inner world and expressing their thoughts and feelings through art and writing.

The Red Book was created during a pivotal period in Jung's life, spanning from 1913 to 1930, when he was grappling with intense personal and professional challenges. During this time, Jung was experiencing profound inner turmoil and vivid, symbolic dreams.

To make sense of his inner world and navigate the turbulent waters of his own psyche, he embarked on a process of active imagination and self-analysis. The result was this unique journal, which he filled with elaborate and intricate drawings, calligraphy and text.

Similar to Freud's technique, clients are asked to respond with the first word that comes to mind when presented with a series of words or images. This can help uncover hidden associations and unconscious thought patterns.

Clients may be asked to identify recurring archetypal themes or figures in their life, such as the hero, shadow, anima/animus, and the wise old man/woman. They can then explore how these archetypes manifest in their personal experiences and relationships.

They can also create mandalas, which are circular images representing wholeness. The process of creating a mandala can help individuals bridge their inner self with an external medium and gain insights into their current emotional and psychological state. Jung emphasized that what had been given to us by the past is adapted to the possibilities of the future.

Our mind has its history, just as our body has its history. You might be just as astonished that man has an appendix, for instance.

Does he know he ought to have an appendix? He is just born with it ... our unconscious mind, like our body, is a storehouse of relics and memories of the past.

The legacy of Carl Jung is a profound and enduring one. His pioneering work in the field of psychology has left an indelible mark on our understanding of the human psyche, influencing not only the realms of psychoanalysis and therapy but also various aspects of culture and society. Controversial in the eyes of many, insightful in the eyes of others – thought-provoking in all.

His concepts have been used by many people as a guide for personal growth and spiritual development. His emphasis on the integration of the shadow and the process of individuation has inspired many to seek a deeper understanding of themselves and their place in the world. His ideas on the collective unconscious, archetypes and the shadow have become a part of our cultural lexicon.

Jung's exploration of the collective unconscious, archetypes and individuation continues to shape our understanding of identity, personal growth and the interplay between the conscious and unconscious realms. His emphasis on the importance of dreams, symbols and the integration of opposing forces has opened new avenues for self-discovery and self-realization.

> *The shoe that fits one person pinches another; there is no recipe for living that suits all cases.*

Jung's work has also left a lasting impact on the study of religion and spirituality. His understanding of the human psyche as inherently oriented towards meaning and the search for purpose has opened up new avenues for dialogue between psychology and spiritual traditions. To understand ourselves, we have to understand how we relate to the world around us.

Jung posited that the collective unconscious contains universal symbols and themes shared by all human beings across cultures and epochs. Archetypes, representing these universal elements, find expression in religious symbols, myths and rituals. Through the lens of archetypes, Jung provided a framework for understanding the commonality of religious experiences and symbols across diverse cultures.

Religions, according to Jung, tap into the collective unconscious to provide a set of shared symbols and narratives that resonate with deep-seated human psychological patterns. Archetypal images like the hero, the shadow and the wise old man manifest in religious stories, providing a psychological roadmap for individuals to navigate the complexities of existence.

Jung's concept of individuation, the process of becoming one's true and unique self, has profound implications for spirituality. Individuation involves integrating the conscious and unconscious aspects of the psyche, leading to a more authentic and harmonious self. While individuation is a psychological concept, its parallels with spiritual awakening and self-realization are evident.

In the realm of religion, Jung's individuation process challenges individuals to go beyond dogma and institutionalized beliefs, encouraging a personal and transformative encounter with the divine. The journey towards individuation often involves confronting and integrating aspects of the shadow. This mirrors the spiritual quest for self-discovery and the transcendence of egoic limitations, akin to the mystic's journey towards union with the divine.

Jung's conception of God diverges from traditional religious notions, offering a more nuanced and psychologically grounded understanding. He spoke of the 'transcendent function', a process through which the conscious and unconscious elements are reconciled, leading to a higher state of awareness. This transcendent function is not confined to religious experiences but is inherent in various aspects of human life, including art, love and individuation.

Jung's idea of the transcendent function resonates with the mystical traditions of various religions, where direct experiences of the divine are often described as transcending ordinary consciousness.

However, Jung's approach is more inclusive, recognizing that such transcendent experiences can occur within the context of everyday life and are not exclusive to religious rituals or doctrines.

With Eastern philosophies, particularly his exploration of the concept of Tao, Jung further enriches his impact on spirituality. The Tao, representing the fundamental principle underlying and unifying the universe in Chinese philosophy, aligns with Jung's emphasis on the integration of opposites. Jung saw parallels between the individuation process and the Eastern notion of balance and harmony, where the reconciliation of opposing forces leads to a state of wholeness.

This integration of Eastern thought into Jungian psychology contributes to a more holistic understanding of spirituality, transcending cultural and religious boundaries. Jung's openness to diverse philosophical traditions encourages individuals to draw wisdom from various sources, fostering a more inclusive and universal spirituality.

Jung's concept of the shadow, the repository of unconscious, repressed or denied aspects of the self, has implications for religious and moral considerations. Engaging with the shadow involves confronting and integrating the darker dimensions of one's psyche, a process that resonates with the themes of sin, repentance and redemption found in many religious traditions.

In religious contexts, the notion of acknowledging and redeeming the shadow aligns with the transformative power of confession, repentance and forgiveness. Jung's emphasis on the importance of facing one's inner darkness contributes to a nuanced understanding of moral and ethical development within a psychological framework.

His impact on religion and spirituality transcends the confines of traditional psychoanalysis, offering a bridge between the psychological and the sacred. His concepts of archetypes, the collective unconscious, individuation, and the transcendent function provide a framework for understanding the profound intersections between psychology and spirituality.

Jung's work encourages a more nuanced, inclusive and psychologically aware approach to religious and spiritual phenomena, fostering a deeper appreciation of the universal aspects of the human experience and the diverse expressions of the sacred across cultures and traditions.

His exploration of the transcendent aspects of human experience has led to fruitful discussions on the intersection of psychology and the numinous. Science and art may be more closely related than we had initially anticipated, according to Jung.

In conclusion, the legacy of Carl Jung's long, highly complex journey, is a testament to the enduring relevance of his ideas and their impact on numerous aspects of human life and culture. Through his pioneering work in analytical psychology, he has provided a framework for exploring the depths of the human mind, inspiring generations of scholars, therapists, artists and individuals on their journeys of self-discovery and personal growth.

Jung's influence extends far beyond the realm of academia, influencing various spheres of society and continuing to shape our understanding of the human experience in profound and meaningful ways. Where would all of our works of art and comprehensive psychotherapy practices be, had the founding father of psychoanalysis been born in another century?

We'll conclude our journey through Jung's life with cheers to his iconic last recorded words to his caregiver, Franziska Baumann: 'Let's have a really good red wine tonight.'

GLOSSARY OF JUNGIAN TERMS

Active imagination: A Jungian technique where an individual engages in a conscious dialogue or creative interaction with elements from their dreams or unconscious, facilitating self-discovery.

Alchemy: Jung used alchemical symbolism as a metaphor for the process of psychological transformation and individuation.

Analytical psychology: A Jungian branch of psychology that explores the unconscious mind, archetypes and individuation. It focuses on dream analysis, persona and shadow integration, and understanding psychological types, fostering self-awareness and personal growth.

Anima/Animus: In a man's psychology, the inner feminine aspect of his psyche. In a woman's psychology, it's called the animus. These represent the contrasexual aspects of an individual's unconscious.

Anima/Animus possession: Anima possession occurs when a man becomes overly identified with or controlled by his anima, leading to irrational emotions and behaviour that are out of touch with reality. Animus possession is where a woman becomes overly influenced by her inner masculine aspect.

Archetypal image: A universal symbol or representation of an archetype, such as the mother, father, hero or wise old man; it appears in myths, dreams and cultural stories.

Archetypal symbolism: The use of archetypal symbols and motifs in literature, art and religion to tap into universal human experiences and themes.

Archetype: The different psychic drivers assigned a particular role behind human *motivation*.

Cognitive functions: A set of eight behaviour-based 'building blocks' that make up the differences between the 16 Jungian personality types.

Collective unconscious: A pool of psychic images and knowledge known to everyone, which is present at birth. They include Jung's archetypes, which are present in dreams.

Complex: A core pattern of emotions, memories and desires organized around a particular theme, often rooted in personal experiences.

Consciousness expansion: The result of successful individuation, where an individual's awareness and understanding of themselves and the world around them deepen and broaden.

Dream analysis: The process of interpreting dreams as a means to uncover unconscious material and gain insight into one's psyche.

Ego: Freud's second part to his three-part model of the psyche, responsible for reality. It mediates the decisions of the id and superego.

Ego inflation: A condition where the ego becomes excessively dominant or inflated, leading to a disconnection from the deeper layers of the psyche and potential psychological imbalance.

Ego-syntonic/Ego-dystonic: Ego-syntonic refers to thoughts and behaviours that are in harmony with one's self-image, while ego-dystonic refers to those that are in conflict with one's self-image.

Enantiodromia: The tendency of things to turn into their opposites, suggesting that extreme attitudes or behaviours may eventually flip into their polar opposites over time.

Extraversion (E): The inclination to gain energy around other people and be preoccupied with the external world.

Extraverted Feeling (Fe): One of Jung's eight functions that deals with the external world. **Connecting** → Harmonizing with other people to feel a warm togetherness.

Extraverted Intuition (Ne): One of Jung's eight functions that deals with the external world. **Brainstorming** → Coming up with many possibilities of the future for numerous projects at once.

Extraverted Sensing (Se): One of Jung's eight functions that deals with the external world. **Experiencing** → Soaking in each moment through all five senses.

Extraverted Thinking (Te): One of Jung's eight functions that deals with the external world. **Evaluating** → Organizing a workday through schedules and tasks to maximize efficiency.

Feeling (F): The preference to make decisions based on how they'll affect other people, personal (subjective) values, and how one 'feels' towards the situation.

Four Humours: Hippocrates' theory of personality imbalance due to bodily fluids, namely Sanguine (blood), Choleric (yellow bile), Phlegmatic (phlegm) and Melancholic (black bile).

I Ching: Ancient Chinese divination text and philosophical treatise. Composed of a collection of symbols called hexagrams, which are formed by combining solid and broken lines. These hexagrams represent various situations, archetypal forces and patterns of change that reflect the dynamic nature of the universe and human experience.

Id: The childlike and impulsive core of Freud's three-part model of the psyche, responsible for biological urges such as hunger and thirst.

Imago: In the context of relationships, imago refers to the unconscious image of a significant figure from early life, influencing one's choice of partners and dynamics in relationships.

Individuation: The process of becoming one's true and unique self by integrating the various aspects of the unconscious into conscious awareness. It's a central goal in Jungian psychology.

Inferiority complex: A psychological condition characterized by feelings of inadequacy and low self-esteem. Jung explored the idea that this complex can be related to the underdeveloped aspects of the personality.

Inflation: A state of excessive self-importance or identification with the persona, often resulting in a loss of contact with the deeper aspects of the self. It can lead to psychological imbalance.

Introversion (I): The inclination to gain energy alone and be preoccupied with the internal world of thoughts, ideas and feelings.

Introverted Feeling (Fi): One of Jung's eight functions that deals with the internal world. **Internalizing** → Understanding internal feelings to achieve value congruence and authenticity with actions.

Introverted Intuition (Ni): One of Jung's eight functions that deals with the internal world. **Envisioning** → Picturing the future and how it'll look from the inside out.

Introverted Sensing (Si): One of Jung's eight functions that deals with the internal world. **Recalling** → Remembering past details and comparing them to the present.

Introverted Thinking (Ti): One of Jung's eight functions that deals with the internal world. **Understanding** → Gathering data and theories to formulate a complete idea of a concept.

Intuition (N): The preference for hunches, 'a-ha!' moments and knowing through information and 'what could be' in terms of ideas.

Judging (J): The preference to meet (sometimes beat) deadlines, schedule events in advance, and view time as a finite (and important) resource.

Likert scale: Linear set of responses with increasing or decreasing intensity, often ranging with options from *Strongly Disagree* to *Strongly Agree*.

Mandala: A circular or geometric pattern often used as a symbol of the self and the process of individuation.

Neurosis: Jung's term for abnormal psychological processing after trauma. It's now more commonly known as mental illness. He coined the term after being pushed to the ground and experiencing seizures.

Perceiving (P): The preference to keep options open 'in case' something better comes along, see deadlines as flexible, and view time as an elastic resource.

Persona: The 'social mask' people wear in public to conceal certain parts of the true self, comparable to Freud's ego and superego.

Persona dissolution: The breakdown or deconstruction of the social mask (persona), often experienced during moments of crisis or profound personal transformation.

Persona shadow: The aspect of the shadow that contains the qualities and traits an individual represses or hides to conform to societal expectations.

Personality: An umbrella term for the traits, behaviours and preferences of an individual that stays *relatively consistent* over the course of time.

Personality trait: A characteristic or quality of an individual that distinguishes their character.

Personality type: A wrapped psychological box of personality traits that result in a select few types. Jung's theory resulted in 16 different personality types.

Projection: Unconsciously attributing one's own thoughts, feelings or traits to another person or object. Projection often involves projecting aspects of the personal unconscious on to others.

Psychic energy: The dynamic and motivating force behind psychological processes, according to Jung's theories, which can be redirected and transformed through self-awareness and individuation.

Psychoid: A hypothetical borderland between the psyche and the outer world, suggesting a bridge between the inner and outer realities.

Psychology: The study of human behaviour and how we think, act and feel.

Psychological complexes: Subsets of the personal unconscious that contain emotionally charged memories and experiences related to a specific theme, often influencing one's thoughts and behaviours.

Psychological integration: The ongoing process of harmonizing and balancing the various elements of the psyche, including the conscious and unconscious aspects, to achieve greater wholeness.

Psychological resilience: The ability to cope with and adapt to life's challenges, often enhanced through the process of individuation and self-awareness.

Psychological shadow integration: The deliberate effort to explore and embrace the shadow, integrating its contents into conscious awareness to achieve greater self-understanding and personal growth.

Psychological types: Jung's theory that individuals can be categorized into different personality types based on their preferences for functions such as thinking, feeling, sensing and intuiting.

Psychometrics: The scientific design of personality tests to measure traits, as well as the interpretation of those collected results.

Psychopomp: A mediator or guide between the conscious and unconscious realms, often represented in dreams or myths as a character like Hermes or a shamanic figure.

Psychosis: A severe mental disorder where an individual loses touch with reality, often associated with a fragmentation of the psyche.

Puer/Puella aeternus: Archetypal representations of eternal youth, symbolizing the desire to remain forever young and avoid the responsibilities and challenges of adulthood.

***Red Book*:** Carl Jung's personal journal and artistic work, which contains his exploration of the unconscious and symbolic images.

Self: The central and unifying archetype that represents the totality of the psyche, including the conscious and unconscious aspects. It's often depicted as a circle or mandala.

Self-realization: The ultimate goal of individuation, where an individual becomes fully aware of and integrates all aspects of the self, leading to a more complete and authentic life.

Sensing (S): The preference to take in information through the five senses: sight, touch, taste, hearing and smell; knowing through doing.

Shadow: The dark and unconscious aspect of one's personality, containing repressed weaknesses, desires and instincts. It's often seen as the opposite of the ego.

Shadow projection: The tendency to project one's own repressed qualities, desires or traits on to others, often leading to misunderstandings and conflicts in relationships.

Shadow work: The process of exploring and integrating the shadow aspects of one's personality to achieve greater self-awareness and wholeness.

Shen: Spiritual rising aspect of a person, often associated with consciousness, mind and divine presence. It is considered one of the Three Treasures, along with Jing (essence) and Qi (vital energy).

Superego: The third part to Freud's three-part model of the psyche, responsible for morality and doing what is 'right' in terms of ethics, and depending on the person, religious values. It develops around age 3–5 in children.

Symbolism: The use of symbols and metaphorical imagery in dreams, art and myths as a means for the unconscious to communicate and reveal deeper meaning.

Synchronicity: The concept that meaningful coincidences can occur that connect the individual's inner experiences to external events without a causal relationship.

Syzygy: The union of opposites, often symbolized by the conjunction of masculine and feminine elements in the psyche. It represents a higher level of psychic integration.

Thinking (T): The preference to make decisions based on facts, statistics, pros and cons and objectives.

Transcendent function: The process by which the conscious and unconscious aspects of the psyche are integrated to achieve a higher level of consciousness and self-awareness.

Transpersonal psychology: A field of psychology that explores spiritual and mystical experiences, which can be related to Jungian concepts of the self and individuation.

Unconscious: The part of the psyche that contains thoughts, memories and desires that are not currently in conscious awareness.

Uroboros: A symbol of a serpent or dragon eating its own tail, representing cyclicality, self-sufficiency and the eternal renewal of life. It's often used in Jungian psychology to illustrate the process of psychological transformation.

Visions: In Jungian psychology, visions or dream imagery are seen as important messages from the unconscious and are often analysed for their symbolic content.

Vitalism: The belief in a life force or energy that animates living beings and is considered an important concept in Jung's psychology.

Wholeness: A central concept in Jungian psychology, it refers to the goal of integrating all aspects of the self, including the unconscious, to achieve a sense of completeness and individuation.

Wounded healer: A concept that refers to individuals who have experienced and healed from their own psychological wounds and trauma, enabling them to help others in their healing journey.

Xenogenesis: In Jungian terms, this refers to the process of transformation or rebirth, often associated with individuation.

Xenophobe: This term isn't specifically Jungian, but it could be related to Jungian concepts when considering how the fear of the unknown or the 'other' can manifest in the psyche and influence one's attitudes and behaviours.

Yin and Yang: While not originally Jungian, these Chinese philosophical concepts represent the interplay of opposites, a theme that Jung incorporated into his ideas about the anima and animus.

Yoga: While not inherently Jungian, Jung did explore Eastern philosophies and practices like yoga, and some Jungians have integrated yoga and meditation into their therapeutic approaches.

Zeitgeist: A term used to describe the spirit or cultural climate of a particular time period, which can influence the collective unconscious and shape the symbols and archetypes that emerge in that era.

Zen: Another Eastern philosophy that Jung explored, Zen Buddhism emphasizes mindfulness, meditation and the direct experience of reality, which can align with some aspects of Jungian psychology.

BIBLIOGRAPHY

Anton, Andreas & Schellinger, Uwe & Wittmann, Marc. (2021). 'It is all so Strangely Intertwined.' A discussion between Hans Bender and Carl Gustav Jung about synchronicity (1960). Phanês 4, 1–50. *Phanês Journal For Jung History*. 4. 1–50. https://doi.org/10.32724/phanes.2021.schellinger.et.al.

Barreto, M.H. (2018). The ethical dimension of analytical psychology. *The Journal of Analytical Psychology*, 63(2), 241–254. https://doi.org/10.1111/1468-5922.12396.

Baum, Rob. (2018). A Walk on the Beach with Jung: Active Imagination and the Quantum Realm. *Jung Journal*. 12. 73–87. https://doi.org/10.1080/19342039.2018.1512349.

Boccassini, Daniela. (2019). Down to the Father's Womb: Jung's and Dante's Encounters with the Dead. *Jung Journal*. 13. 46–81. https://doi.org/10.1080/19342039.2019.1600994.

Bray, Carolyn & Healy, Nan Savage. (2020). *Toni Wolff & C.G. Jung: A Collaboration*. Los Angeles: Tiberius. 2017. pp. xi + 402. Pbk. n.p. *Journal of Analytical Psychology*. 65. 235–238. https://doi.org/10.1111/1468-5922.12557.

Brooke, Roger. (2019). Jung's Fantasies of Africa and Africa's Healing of Analytical Psychology. *International Journal of Jungian Studies*. 11. 1–20. https://doi.org/10.1163/19409060-01101003.

Buck, Stephanie. (2018). Hiding in plain sight: Jung, astrology, and the psychology of the unconscious. *Journal of Analytical Psychology*. 63. 207–227. https://doi.org/10.1111/1468-5922.12394.

Buckle, Pamela. (2022). The Anthropocene as Symbol: Imagined Through Jung's Answer to Job. *International Journal of Jungian Studies*. 15. 1–28. https://doi.org/10.1163/19409060-bja10013.

Bushueva, Tatyana. (2019). C. Jung Theory Of Unconscious And Literary Text. 544–553. https://doi.org/10.15405/epsbs.2019.12.04.74.

Cassar, Laner. (2020). Jung's Technique of Active Imagination and Desoille's Directed Waking Dream Method: Bridging the Divide. https://doi.org/10.4324/9780429454394.

Cohen, Betsy. (2020). Jung's Personal Confession. *Jung Journal*. 14. 44–71. https://doi.org/10.1080/19342039.2020.1822119.

Cornelissen, Matthijs. (2018). The Self and the Structure of the Personality: An Overview of Sri Aurobindo's Topography of Consciousness. *International Journal of Transpersonal Studies*. 37. 63–89. https://doi.org/10.24972/ijts.2018.37.1.63.

Davis, Judson. (2020). Active Imagination in Psychotherapy. https://doi.org/10.1007/978-3-642-27771-9_200208-2.

Dib, Roula-Maria. (2019). The Love-Hate Relationship between Jung and Modern Art. *International Journal of Jungian Studies*. 13. 1–12. https://doi.org/10.1163/19409060-01101008.

Erazo Andrade, Santiago & Masunah, Juju & Milyartini, Rita. (2022). Art Creation Using Active Imagination To Express Collective Unconsciousness. https://doi.org/10.54808/WMSCI2022.03.1.

Etter, Hansueli. (2020). Synchronicity and 'Being Endowed with Meaning'. *Psychological Perspectives*. 63. 106–117. https://doi.org/10.1080/00332925.2020.1739469.

Fierro, Catriel. (2022). How Did Early North American Clinical Psychologists Get Their First Personality Test? Carl Gustav Jung, The Zurich School of Psychiatry and The Development of the 'Word Association Test' (1898–1909). *History of Psychology*. 25. 295–321. https://doi.org/10.1037/hop0000218.

Furnham, Adrian & McClelland, Alastair. (2022). Folk Concepts and Jung: The Relationship between the California Personality Inventory (CPI) and the MBTI. *Psychology*. 13. 829–841. 10.4236/psych.2022.135056.

Giles, David. (2020). A Typology of Persona as Suggested by Jungian Theory and the Evolving Persona Studies Literature. *Persona Studies*. 6. 15–29. https://doi.org/10.21153/psj2020vol6no1art997.

Hamer, Marc & Collins, Jan. (2019). *Romantic Love Songs and the Transcendent Function*. New York: Quadrant: *Journal of the C. G. Jung Foundation*. XLIX:1. pp. 38–50.

Han, Youngsue. (2019). Jungian Character Network in Growing Other Character Archetypes in Films. 15. 13–19. https://doi.org/10.5392/IJoC.2019.15.2.013.

Harris, James. (2021). Psychedelic-Assisted Psychotherapy and Carl Jung's Red Book. *JAMA Psychiatry*. 78. https://doi.org/10.1001/jamapsychiatry.2021.1207.

Hunziker, M., & Dunlap, P.T. (2021). Embodying the psychological attitude: types of consciousness in the transformation of culture. *The Journal of Analytical Psychology*, 66(5), 1177–1205. https://doi.org/10.1111/1468-5922.12735.

Johnson J. (2020). Being white, being Jungian: implications of Jung's encounter with the 'non-European' other. *The Journal of Analytical Psychology*, 65(4), 707–718. https://doi.org/10.1111/1468-5922.12619.

Korkunova, Olga & Bushueva, Tatyana. (2019). Philosophical Discourse in Psychology of C. Jung. SHS Web of Conferences. 72. 03028. 10.1051/shsconf/20197203028.

Kroeker, Joel. (2019). Jungian Music Psychotherapy: When Psyche Sings. https://doi.org/10.4324/9780429459740.

Lemos, Pan. (2020). The glow of Telesphorus: a brief enquiry into the sense of the term 'mana personality' and the dynamic of experiences behind it. *Journal of Analytical Psychology*. 65. 890–910. https://doi.org/10.1111/1468-5922.12633.

Liebscher, Martin. (2020). C.G. Jung and the Berneuchen Movement: Meditation and Active Imagination in Jungian Psychotherapy and Protestant Spiritual Practice in the 1930s. https://doi.org/10.14324/111.9781787357716.

Lukacs, Orsolya. (2019). Carl Gustav Jung and Albert Einstein: An ambivalent relationship. *Journal of the History of the Behavioral Sciences*. 56. https://doi.org/10.1002/jhbs.22014.

Mahr, G. & Drake, C.L. (2022). Singing in tune: Carl Jung and The Red Book. Sleep health, 8(4), 347–349. https://doi.org/10.1016/j.sleh.2022.06.003.

Marlan, Stanton. (2020). The metaphor of light and its deconstruction in Jung's alchemical vision. https://doi.org/10.4324/9780429356513-7.

McGovern, H.T. & Hutchinson, Brendan & Wells, Emma & Bandara, Kavindu & Foe, Alexander. (2023). Constructing Representations: Jungian Archetypes and the Free Energy Principle. https://doi.org/10.31234/osf.io/ygptv.

Mills, J. (2019). Jung and Philosophy. https://doi.org/10.4324/9780429261763.

Mills, Jon. (2012). Jung's Metaphysics. *International Journal of Jungian Studies*. 5. 1–25. https://doi.org/10.1080/19409052.2012.671182.

Miller, Juliet. (2020). Art, Memoir and Jung: Personal and Psychological Encounters. https://doi.org/10.4324/9781003083030.

Mlisa, Lily Rose. (2020). Encountering the other: Jungian analysts and traditional healers in South Africa Part III: The traditional health practitioner's stance and the world view. *Journal of Analytical Psychology*. 65. 212–215. https://doi.org/10.1111/1468-5922.12564.

Morbach, A.C.B. & Pedroso, J.D.S. (2022). Aspects of the development of older adults in the perspective of analytical psychology: a systematic review of qualitative findings. *Aging & mental health*, 26(1), 1–12. https://doi.org/10.1080/13607863.2020.1849024.

Murphy, Elizabeth. (2021). Type development in childhood and beyond. *Journal of Analytical Psychology*. 66. 1074–1093. https://doi.org/10.1111/1468-5922.12730.

Nash, George & Children, George & Merritt, Dennis. (2021). Sacred Landscapes, Sacred Seasons: A Jungian Ecopsychological Perspective.

Pylkkö, P. (2019). Ambiguity and contradiction: the outlines of Jung's dialectics. *The Journal of Analytical Psychology*, 64(5), 823–844. https://doi.org/10.1111/1468-5922.12548.

Roesler, Christian. (2019). Theoretical foundations of analytical psychology: recent developments and controversies. *Journal of Analytical Psychology*. 64. 658–681. https://doi.org/10.1111/1468-5922.12540.

Roesler, C. & Reefschläger, G.I. (2022). Jungian psychotherapy, spirituality, and synchronicity: Theory, applications, and evidence base. *Psychotherapy* (Chicago, Ill.), 59(3), 339–350. https://doi.org/10.1037/pst0000402.

Roesler, Christian & Ulyet, Alexander. (2021). C.G. Jung's Archetype Concept: Theory, Research and Applications. https://doi.org/10.4324/9781003058458.

Rowland, Susan A. & Weishaus, Joel. (2020). Jung and arts-based research. https://doi.org/10.4324/9780429459238-1.

Schwartz, Susan. (2022). Puer Shadow. https://doi.org/10.13140/RG.2.2.21359.30887.

Sharma, Manoj. (2019). Jung's Collective Unconscious, Integrative (Mind-Body-Spirit) Yoga, and Self-Realization. https://doi.org/10.4018/978-1-5225-9065-1.ch005.

Sorge, Giovanni. (2020). The theory of the 'mana personality' in Jung's works: a historic–hermeneutic perspective. Part II. *Journal of Analytical Psychology*. 65. 519–537. https://doi.org/10.1111/1468-5922.12598.

Swan-Foster, Nora. (2020). C.G. Jung's Influence on Art Therapy and the Making of the Third. *Psychological Perspectives*, 63:1, 67–94, https://doi.org/10.1080/00332925.2020.1739467.

Tozzi C. (2020). From horror to ethical responsibility: Carl Gustav Jung and Stephen King encounter the dark half within us, between us and in the world. *The Journal of Analytical Psychology*, 65(1), 219–234. https://doi.org/10.1111/1468-5922.12567.

Trzeciak Huss, Joanna. (2021). From E.E. to Erna Eltzner: Tokarczuk,

Jung and the Ethics of Care. *The Polish Review*. 66. 1–23. https://doi.org/10.5406/polishreview.66.3.0003.

Turchin, Alexey. (2021). Jungian Active Imagination as an Alternative to Lucid Dreaming: Theory and Experimental Results. https://doi.org/10.13140/RG.2.2.26538.54724.

Vestergaard, A. & Odde, D. (2021). Jungian socioanalysis, social dreaming and the emerging complexity of Europe. *The Journal of Analytical Psychology*, 66(2), 323–344. https://doi.org/10.1111/1468-5922.12668.

Waite, Libby. (2021). 'Who Am I Really?': Jung, Yoga, and Embodied Individuation: An Ethnographic Exploration of the Transcultural Journey to the Self. *International Journal of Jungian Studies*. 14. 1–29. https://doi.org/10.1163/19409060-bja10014.

Wertz, Frederick. (2020). Jung's break with Freud revisited: Research method and the character of theory in psychoanalysis.

Young, Willow. (2020). Eros and the Value of Relatedness: The Lineage of an Enduring Friendship between Carl Jung and Ochwiay Biano. *Psychological Perspectives*, 63:3-4, 441–457. https://doi.org/10.1080/00332925.2020.1898853.

Zwart, Hub. (2019). Archetypes of Knowledge: The Relevance of Jung's Psychology of Scientific Discovery for Understanding Contemporary Technoscience. *International Journal of Jungian Studies*. 2019. 1–21. https://doi.org/10.1163/19409060-01102005.

INDEX